Critical Literacy

Enhancing Students' Comprehension of Text

MAUREEN MCLAUGHLIN
GLENN L. DEVOOGD

FOREWORD BY ALLAN LUKE

SCHOLASTIC

NEW YORK • TORONTO • LONDON • AUCKLAND • SYDNEY
MEXICO CITY • NEW DELHI • HONG KONG • BUENOS AIRES

Dedication

◆ ·································· ◆

For Marian and Jack McGraw
—MM

For my parents,
Lawrence and Ursula DeVoogd,
who taught me that
love is an action word.
—GLD

Cover and interior design by Maria Lilja
Cover photo © by Vicki Kasala
Copyedited by Jeannie Hutchins

ISBN: 0-439-62804-0
Copyright © 2004 by Maureen McLaughlin and Glenn L. DeVoogd
All rights reserved. Published by Scholastic Inc.
Printed in the U.S.A.

5 6 7 8 9 10   23   10 09 08 07 06

Contents

Foreword

The teaching of literacy is not neutral—it is not a matter of universal skills or "natural" processes. Each day our teaching involves the selection and framing of values, ideologies, and contending versions of "truth." In every classroom, teachers make decisions about how to shape the attitudes and stances that kids will learn to take towards the writing, the images, the narratives, the media that make up the fabric of everyday life in information and text-saturated societies and cultures.

If you thought our work was about phonics or about inculcating a love of children's literature—or that literacy education is simply a matter of finding the most scientific approach to teaching and learning—Maureen McLaughlin and Glenn DeVoogd have some surprises in store for you. Their work here aims to change the way you think about literacy, about your students' lives and their textual worlds. Throughout they offer strategies and practices that will enable you to teach with new force and relevance.

For those of us who have worked with issues of critical literacy for the last several decades, it has always been about teaching kids to read not as passive recipients or processors of knowledge, not as "sponges" who would uncritically learn to love the literature or the advertisements or media reports presented to them, but as readers who would continually use power against, with, and along with power. As a teacher educator I have always contested the view that children should "learn to love books": indeed, books can deceive, delude, and misrepresent, as readily as they can enlighten and expand our knowledge. Accordingly, many of the approaches to teaching that are introduced in this volume act as a balance against current approaches to teaching literature—recognizing that literacy and access to print can act as a double-edged sword, disenabling as readily as enabling, deceiving as readily as enlightening.

In this way, critical literacy is necessarily abrasive; it involves second guessing, reading against the grain, asking hard and harder questions, seeing underneath, behind, and beyond texts, trying to see and "call" how these texts establish and use power over us, over others, on whose behalf, in whose interests. Those students that I and others working in Australia, Canada, the UK, and the US have taught—whether adult migrant learners, student teachers, or primary school children—often come back to us and say, "You've messed me up forever. I can never read a label, advertisement, or headline without second guessing it, without asking what it's trying to do to me."

As McLaughlin and DeVoogd here point out, the basis for critical literacy can be traced most directly to the work of Paulo Freire in the 1960s. The project of critical literacy as framed by Freire is about teaching "readings of the world" and thereby socially repositioning learners. For Freire this meant understanding what words meant, how they were used as tools to do things in institutions, to societies and cultures. This means learning to ask serious questions about the authority of these words, about the apparent power and magic they have over our lives. This isn't easy stuff—because it means a commitment to a kind of education that is about destabilizing knowledge, as much as it might be about establishing it—about taking things apart and understanding how and in what institutional contexts and interests they work, as much as it might about putting them together.

Perhaps we couldn't always see this clearly as long as we were primarily a print-born generation of baby-boomer teachers, carefully producing and reproducing the genres and the values, the plays and novels, that had been taught to us. Perhaps it took a universe of wall-to-wall cable, of redundant, powerful, and complex images in cyberspace, of an infinitely expanding online archive of truth and lies, of realities and simulations, of authentic identities and frauds, to awaken us to the fact that all that is written and presented to us cannot be taken for granted as reliable, dependable, in our interests.

Reading this book, it might be tempting to simply say "too hard," or that this is all too political—to retreat to the safe haven of belief that teaching is just about kids, books, and skills. But every day that we teach we in fact make choices; we make decisions about which texts, which messages, which values, and which attitudes we represent towards the truths of texts and discourses.

There is no magic method for literacy. There is no single or simple or unified approach to critical literacy on offer here. Ultimately, neither Glenn DeVoogd nor Maureen McLaughlin can tell us which choices—which texts and skills, knowledges and ideologies are the right ones to teach. For they necessarily are every teacher's ethical and moral, social and cultural choices. And that may be what sets approaches to critical literacy apart—they don't purport to provide a universal, incontestable, scientific answer about how to teach. Instead, they very deliberately open up a universe of possibilities, of possible critical readings, critical reading positions and practices. The rest, simply, is up to you and your own "reading of the world."

Allan Luke

National Institute of Education, Singapore

Introduction

When you were in school, did you believe everything you read? We did. We never questioned who was writing the text, who was determining what topics would be included in it, or who was deciding what would be excluded from it. We never questioned if there was any perspective other than the one presented in the daily newspaper, on the evening news, or in our textbooks. We were passive recipients of knowledge. Critical literacy helps us to move beyond that passive acceptance and take an active role in the reader-author relationship by questioning issues such as who wrote the text, what the author wanted us to believe, and what information the author chose to include or exclude in the text. For example, if we had been reading from a critical perspective when we were students, we would have questioned whether the whole story about Columbus's explorations was included in the text (we now know that the true story extended well beyond what was included in the textbooks), whether historical events such as World War II were presented from multiple perspectives (e.g., victims of the Holocaust, women working on the home front, children, or citizens of various countries who worked to save Jewish people), or whether genders and minorities were represented in equal ways (we now know that the list of great inventors extends beyond white men).

Critical literacy helps us to read texts in deeper, more meaningful ways. It encourages readers of all ages to become actively engaged and use their power to construct understanding and not be used by the text to fulfill the intentions of the author. It helps readers understand that there are many ways of thinking about and understanding a topic and that the author has explained it in only one way.

We need critical literacy because it helps us: (1) to establish equal status in the reader-author relationship; (2) to understand the motivation the author had for writing the text (the function) and how the author uses the text to make us understand in a particular way (the form); (3) to understand that the author's perspective is not the only perspective; and (4) to become active users of the information in texts to develop independent perspectives, as opposed to being passive reproducers of the ideas in texts.

Current thinking about reading comprehension supports the idea that critical literacy enhances readers' understanding. It suggests that we can extend our traditional definition of comprehension to understand the author's message beyond what appears on the printed page—to comprehend from a critical stance. This critical awareness deepens readers' comprehension of text by enabling them to become actively engaged with the text and question the author's purpose, thinking, and format. It relates to the reading of traditional print formats, such as books, newspapers, and magazines, but also extends to hypertext, music, movies, conversations and everyday situations.

In this book, we examine critical literacy from the perspectives of both theory and practice in grades K–8. We begin with a discussion of critical theory and explain a variety of critical literacy strategies and their implementation. We provide responses to questions often raised by educators seeking to integrate critical literacy into their teaching. These include:

◆ What is critical literacy?

◆ How does it help readers to deepen their comprehension?

◆ How does it function within current beliefs about literacy?

◆ How does it fit into school curriculums and support state standards?

◆ How can we become critically aware?

◆ How can we teach our students to become critically aware?

We respond to these queries by providing a clear, practical understanding of critical literacy and all that it entails, while simultaneously acknowledging that every critical literacy experience is innately unique.

We have developed this book as a focused and easily accessed teachers' resource. In Part One, we present the theoretical underpinnings of critical literacy, define it, and explain the role it plays in deepening readers' understanding of text. Next, we explain the importance of reading from a critical stance and delineate the principles of critical literacy. Then, we discuss ideas for teaching critical literacy and present instructional frameworks and a variety of critical literacy strategies.

Part Two describes critical literacy in action at the primary, intermediate, and middle school levels. It contains teacher-designed, classroom-taught lessons based on three themes: Challenging the Text, Exploring Identities, and Seeing Beyond the Bias. The teaching framework for these lessons focuses on engaging, guiding, and extending students' thinking. Teacher commentaries and examples of student work, including written responses, sketches, dramatization, and song lyrics, are featured throughout this section. The final chapter contains teacher and student reflections on critical literacy that delineate what being critically aware means to them.

The book concludes with three appendices. The first is a glossary of critical literacy terms; the second is an extensive, annotated list of trade books to use when teaching critical literacy; and the third is an annotated list of websites that either provide further information about critical literacy or serve as resources for developing critical literacy lessons about a variety of issues.

Research supports that reading from a critical stance adds a new dimension of understanding. We wrote this book to offer you a practical guide to that dimension— one that explores the ideas and strategies that take us beyond reading comprehension as we have known it and provides practical ideas for teaching and learning from a critical perspective.

Acknowledgments

Creating this book has been a collaborative effort. We extend our gratitude to all who contributed to the manuscript's development, especially the classroom teachers who inspired this volume. We also offer special thanks to the following:

The primary, intermediate, and middle school teachers who contributed lessons and student work:

Leslie Fisher, Franklin Elementary School, Roxbury School District, Roxbury, New Jersey

Karolyn Martin, Kennedy Elementary School, Roxbury School District, Roxbury, New Jersey

Amy Homeyer, Lincoln Roosevelt Elementary School, Roxbury School District, Roxbury, New Jersey

Jennifer Sassaman, Lincoln Roosevelt Elementary School, Roxbury School District, Roxbury, New Jersey

Mary Roehrenbeck, Asa Packer Elementary School, Bethlehem Area School District, Bethlehem, Pennsylvania

Denise Adamoyurka, Washington Irving Middle School, Fairfax County Public Schools, Springfield, Virginia

Susan Sillivan, East Hills Middle School, Bethlehem Area School District, Bethlehem, Pennsylvania

Belinda Anderson, Bangor Area Middle School, Bangor Area School District, Bangor, Pennsylvania

Kathy Franson, Tenaya Middle School, Fresno, California

Kristina Karlson, Richmond Elementary School, Hanford, California

Scott Johnson, Daily Elementary School, Fresno, California

Donna Seward, Raison City Middle School, Raison City, California

Kimber Pauls, Golden Valley School, Orosi, California

Denise White, Wilson Elementary School, Sanger, California

Cathleen Perez, Wilson Elementary School, Sanger, California

Our colleagues, especially those who have written about critical literacy, who inspire our research and writing;

Allan Luke for sharing his in-depth knowledge of critical literacy and for writing the foreword to our work;

Family and friends, who demonstrated extraordinary patience and encouraged us throughout the researching and writing of this volume;

Our graduate and undergraduate students, including Denise Delp, Molly Brundage, Dana Turney, Stacey Sharek, and Kelly-Jo Smith;

Victoria and Sarah Principe;

The staff at the Arne Nixon Center for the Study of Children's Literature at California State University, Fresno;

Margery Rosnick, Acquisitions Editor, Scholastic;

Ray Coutu, Ellen Dreyer, and Bernice Golden for reading and commenting on the manuscript;

And, finally, we thank you, our readers, for your interest in learning about critical literacy. We hope you will find this volume to be a practical and valuable guide for your journey toward critical awareness.

—MM & GLD

Demystifying Critical Literacy

Before we, as teachers, can begin to use critical literacy, we need to have a clear understanding of what it is and why it is important. Once we become critically aware, we need to know how to teach our students to read from a critical stance. These are the topics addressed in Part One.

In Chapter 1, we define critical literacy, discuss related principles, and examine how critical literacy relates to current beliefs about literacy. Then, we discuss how critical literacy supports state standards and functions within school curriculums.

In Chapter 2, we focus on creating contexts that promote critical literacy. Ideas that support critical literacy, instructional frameworks, critical literacy strategies, and texts are among the topics addressed.

CHAPTER 1

Becoming Critically Aware

"Critical literacy has opened up a new level of understanding to my students and to me. In the past, we were very focused on comprehension, but now it is that and more. It's as if comprehension used to be our ultimate goal, but now it's the point at which we begin our critical discussions."

AMY HOMEYER, fifth grade teacher

Amy is a member of a group of educators we've been working with who have been infusing critical literacy into their teaching for the past two years. As you'll read in subsequent chapters, other members of the group have also commented on their students' ability to comprehend at deeper levels—levels that go beyond the usual goal of understanding the text to understanding from a critical perspective.

Current thinking about reading (Luke & Freebody, 1999; Pearson, 2001) suggests that we should help our students to comprehend at these deeper levels—levels that require them to think beyond the information on the printed page and critically analyze the author's message. Reading from a critical perspective involves thinking beyond the text to understand issues such as why the author wrote about a particular topic, wrote from a particular perspective, or chose to include some ideas about the topic and exclude others.

In this chapter, we examine critical literacy by responding to a number of frequently asked questions. We begin by explaining what critical literacy is, discussing related principles, and making connections to current beliefs about literacy. Next, we explain how critical literacy fits into school curriculums and supports state standards. Finally, we discuss how we, as teachers, can use our understanding of critical literacy to help our students become critically literate.

What Is Critical Literacy?

Critical literacy views readers as active participants in the reading process and invites them to move beyond passively accepting the text's message to question, examine, or dispute the power relations that exist between readers and authors. It focuses on issues of power and promotes reflection, transformation, and action (Freire, 1970).

THE PRINCIPLES OF CRITICAL LITERACY

The Principles of Critical Literacy (McLaughlin & DeVoogd, 2004) include a number of essential understandings and beliefs about the power relationship that exists between the reader and the author. The four principles follow:

Critical literacy focuses on issues of power and promotes reflection, transformation, and action.

Whenever readers commit to understanding a text—whether narrative or expository—they submit to the right of the author to select the topic and determine the treatment of the ideas. For example, if we, as teachers, read a headline that says, "New Security Standards for Schools Cause Tax-Rate Increase," we would recognize the power of the author of the article to name the problem and determine and express what he perceives to be the negative effects of increased security standards. In turn, we, as readers, may use our power to question that perspective and engage in *reflection* about whose voice might be missing, discounted, or silenced in the article. As a result, we might choose to represent the alternative view of the subordinated group—the schools—and change the title of the text to "Additional Security Measures Provide Greater Protection for Our Children." The readers draw from their background knowledge to create this *transformation*, which might result in taking an action such as writing a letter to the editor of the local newspaper or speaking to a group about the importance of school security. In addition, the readers may also gain a new appreciation of the effect of perspective in writing or even a new understanding of the possible positive costs of increased security. This is an example of how critical literacy focuses on issues of power and helps subjugated or oppressed groups, in this case the teachers, to help "politicize themselves and engage in action aimed at challenging existing structures of inequality and oppression" (Cummins & Sayers, 1995, p. 23). "The challenge is to adopt practices that will not only open up new possibilities but also will begin to deal with taking action" (O'Brien, 2001, p. 53). Good intentions or awareness of an unjust situation will not transform it. We must act on our knowledge.

This cycle of "reflection and action upon the world in order to transform it" is what Freire (1970, p. 36) calls praxis. By nature, this process is not passive but active, challenging and disrupting the ideal (Green, 2001) or commonplace (Lewison, Flint, & Van Sluys, 2002) for the purpose of relieving inequity and injustice.

Critical literacy focuses on the problem and its complexity.

Educational situations that are fairly intricate are often viewed from an essentialist—very simplistic—perspective. In critical literacy, rather than accepting an essentialist view, we would engage in problematizing—seeking to understand the problem and its complexity. In other words, we would raise questions and seek alternative explanations as a way of more fully acknowledging and understanding the complexity of the situation. For example, it would be essentialist to merely suggest that unmotivated students should receive an extrinsic reward for reading or be punished for not reading. Problematizing—or examining the complexity of this situation—would reveal that the lack of motivation is likely due to a variety of factors that may include poor-quality texts, students' past reading experiences, classroom climate, self-efficacy, purpose, or limited opportunities to self-select, read, and discuss books in social settings.

Critical literacy strategies are dynamic and adapt to the contexts in which they are used.

There is no list of methods in critical literacy that work the same way in all contexts all the time. No technique that promotes critical literacy can be exported to another setting without adapting it to that context. As Freire (1998, p. xi) has observed, "It is impossible to export pedagogical practices without reinventing them."

Comber (2001b, p. 271) has observed that when teachers and students are engaged in critical literacy, they "ask complicated questions about language and power, about people and lifestyle, about morality and ethics, and about who is advantaged by the way things are and who is disadvantaged". In order to participate in such a classroom environment readers must play not only the roles of code breakers, meaning makers, and text users, but also the role of text critics (Luke & Freebody, 1999). In other words, readers need to understand that they have the power to envision alternate ways of viewing the author's topic, and they exert that power when they read from a critical stance.

In any exploration of critical literacy, the teacher should constantly assess student responses to ensure that the experience is true to the philosophy and goals of critical literacy, although perhaps not consistent with the examples of others who practice critical literacy. For example, teachers may begin using an approach to critical literacy that is presented here or that they have seen working in another classroom, but upon reflecting on instructional goals and on what is happening in their classes, they may adapt the method to make it more applicable—more meaningful—in that particular context. The dynamic nature of critical literacy supports this type of adaptation. There is a sense of empowerment and confidence in the act of creation that cannot be achieved by copying. Even when a method has already been used, it is never quite the same in future applications. This is why those who are critically aware are fond of quoting Antonio Machado, the Spanish poet, who said, "Caminante, no hay camino, Se hace el camino al andar"— "Traveler, there is no road. The road is made as you walk" (1982, p. 142).

Critical literacy disrupts the commonplace by examining it from multiple perspectives.

Examining the point of view from which a text is written and brainstorming other perspectives that may or may not be represented, challenges students to expand their thinking and discover diverse beliefs, positions, and understandings (McLaughlin, 2001). It helps students to transition from accepting the text at face value to questioning both the author's intent and the information as it is presented in the text. For example, social studies teachers might consider looking at Columbus's explorations from multiple perspectives. In reflecting on whose voices are missing, the class may decide that the perspectives of the Tainos, the people who inhabited the island where Columbus first landed, or Columbus's crew on the final voyage are not represented. Appreciation for and exploration of these alternative perspectives facilitates viewing situations from a critical stance (Lewison et al., 2002; McLaughlin, 2001).

THE RESEARCH BASE

The Principles of Critical Literacy are supported by Lewison, Flint, and Van Sluys' (2002) review of 30 years of professional literature related to critical literacy. The following dimensions emerged from their review:

Disrupting a common situation or understanding—seeking to understand the text or situation in more or less detail to gain perspective.

Example: *Celebrating Ramadan* by Diane Hoyt-Goldsmith is a primary text that disrupts students' understanding of holidays. This text tells about Ibraheem, a New Jersey boy, who disrupts most children's understanding of "religious holiday," which is often limited to Christmas and Hanukkah, by describing this time of peace and harmony for Muslims. At a time when the West is at war in the Middle East, it disrupts the notion that people in the Middle East don't believe in peace.

Scholastic publishes a Dear America series of books that often provide specific details about individuals who have uncommon views. For example, in *Love Thy Neighbor: The Tory Diary of Prudence Emerson*, the reader experiences the tragedies, fears, and hopes of a young American girl during the Revolutionary War. Her family chooses to stay loyal to the King and England instead of joining in a violent revolution. By depicting a loyalist as the main character, this story disrupts the version of the Revolutionary War Americans experience in books, movies, and social studies lessons.

Examining multiple viewpoints—thinking about texts from perspectives of different characters or from perspectives not represented in the texts.

Example: In Faith Ringgold's *If a Bus Could Talk: The Story of Rosa Parks*, readers can examine Rosa Parks's experience on the bus from multiple perspectives, including that of another person riding on the bus, the bus driver, a local citizen, or a member of Rosa Parks's family. When reading informational texts about the Civil War, such as selected letters from Andrew Carroll's *War Letters: Extraordinary Correspondence from American Wars*, readers can examine the perspectives of the recipients of the letters, fellow soldiers, or politicians of the time period.

Focusing on sociopolitical issues—thinking about power in relationships between and among people.

Example: Patricia McKissack's *Christmas in the Big House, Christmas in the Quarters*, another nonfiction book for all ages, recounts the social relationships between the slaves who prepare for both their own celebration in the quarters and their owners' celebration in the big house, in Virginia in 1859. This story helps us see not only the multiple viewpoints of Christmas, but also the differences between the two ethnic groups and the power relationships that sustain the difference.

Taking action and promoting social justice—reflecting and acting to change an inappropriate, unequal power relationship between people.

Example: In a picture-book biography by Molly Bang entitled *Nobody in Particular: One Woman's Fight to Save the Bay*, Diane Wilson, a shrimper, takes on chemical companies whose plants are poisoning the water on the Texas coast where the shrimpers live. This story tells about the many struggles she endured and the costs of taking action.

As you can see from the examples, we don't need to follow the dimensions of critical literacy in sequential order or use them collectively. Whenever we engage in any one of these dimensions, we are engaged in critical literacy. Other examples of the dimensions can be found in the lessons featured in Chapters 3, 4, and 5 and in Appendix B, which contains a wide variety of books to use when teaching critical literacy.

How Does Critical Literacy Relate to Contemporary Beliefs About Literacy?

To understand how critical literacy relates to current beliefs about literacy, we need to begin by exploring the foundational ideas expressed by Paulo Freire (1970) and then make connections to contemporary beliefs, including social constructivism, reading comprehension, context, and reader stance.

FREIRE'S BELIEFS

Paulo Freire, like many people of his time, suffered from the poverty of the Great Depression. He found that education for the common man was not the illuminating experience it was hoped to be. Instead, he learned that education worked to silence the common people, making them feel helpless—like victims who had no control over their lives. To help overcome this, he suggested that people could take the initiative to act and transform their lives and their community through a process of reflection and action.

Although Freire grew up in Brazil, his ideals are represented in the sense of reflection, action, and participation that democratic societies, such as the United States, value. For example, in his "I Have a Dream" speech, Martin Luther King, Jr., stressed the importance of taking political action to achieve equal rights. Freire viewed this type of reflection and action as the essence of our power over our lives.

Freire applies these same beliefs to literacy, suggesting that it should be viewed from a critical stance. In "The Importance of the Act of Reading," Freire (1983) notes that reading is much more than decoding language—it is preceded by and intertwined with knowledge of the world. Because language and reality are dynamically interwoven, the understanding attained by the critical reading of a text implies perceiving the relationship between text and context. Freire suggests that instead of passively accepting the information presented, readers should not only read and understand the word, but "read the world" and understand the text's purpose to avoid being manipulated by it (Freire, 1970). "Reading the world" enables critically aware readers to comprehend beyond the literal level and think about the function and the production of texts. Reading the world means trying to understand what authors are trying to convey in their messages and how they are communicating those messages. It requires that readers not accept superficial responses to the text but rather reflect upon the text's purposes and the author's style. This reasoning is often expressed through dialogue with others who are seeking to understand the hidden forces at work. This kind of reflection takes time and requires constant monitoring of the text.

Reading from this perspective requires both the ability and the deliberate inclination to think critically about—to analyze and evaluate—texts, meaningfully question their origin and purpose, and take action by representing alternative perspectives. It is important to note that critical theorists' expanded notion of texts is not limited to words from a novel, song, or newscast; texts can also be conditions (sociocultural influences, state assessment-driven curriculums, funding or lack of it) or relationships and situations in everyday life (analyzing an occurrence from another person's perspective).

Of course, those of us who grew up in a time of literal-level education remember reading in a very different way. We recall the information sources being the teacher and the text. The standard of success was the ability to give back to the teacher—usually right away—whatever information had been imparted. Because schooling focused on absorbing the maximum number of ideas from the text, the learning experience was a one-way communication from the author to the students, with deference given to the author of the published work. As readers, our ideas were unimportant. It did not matter whether we had had similar experiences, whether we had insights into different perspectives, or whether we wanted to critique the text. We simply didn't have the power. The power to communicate the event belonged to the author. It was the author who set the agenda, established the importance of characters, decided the themes and values discussed, and chose which perspective the information would represent. As readers, we were expected to be passive recipients of information—information which at times was inaccurate or incomplete. In the past, the focus of education was on functional literacy that allowed people to get jobs and be productive.

READING WITH A CRITICAL EDGE

Fortunately, since that time, our understanding of reading has expanded. We have learned, as P. David Pearson (2001) has noted, that "comprehension is never enough; it must have a critical edge." Comprehending with a critical edge means moving beyond understanding the text to understanding the power relationship that exists between the reader and the author—to knowing that even though the author has the power to create and present the message, readers have the power and the right to be text critics, by reading, questioning, and analyzing the author's message. Understanding this power relationship is the essence of critical literacy. To become critically aware, we need to read with a critical edge. We need to refocus. We need to actively engage—to become participants in this power relationship—in order to find new ways of seeing beyond the text, inside the text, and around the text. We need to become text critics. We need to move beyond passively accepting information and, rather, analyze it from a critical perspective. As Van Sluys (2003) observes, "Critical literacy is about the assembly, manipulation, and constant renegotiation of practices that encourage people to become active participants that question how the world is and work toward more just images of what it might be."

Reading as a Thinking Process

To accomplish this, we need to be actively engaged when we read. We need to view comprehension as a strategic thinking process (Durkin, 1978–79) and a social constructivist process. Social constructivists believe that learners make sense of their world by connecting their prior knowledge with what they are learning. Brian Cambourne (2002) notes that constructivism has three core theoretical assumptions: (1) Learning cannot be separated from context; (2) The learner's goals are central to what is learned; and (3) Knowledge and meaning are socially constructed through negotiation, evaluation, and transformation. The personal meaning readers construct may or may not parallel the message the author intended (Harris & Hodges, 1995, p. 39) or the message others construct. The social aspect of constructivism—negotiating meaning with others through discussion or other means—is supported by the work of Lev Vygotsky (1978), who viewed thinking and learning as contextualized social practices.

The Transactional Theory and Reader Stance

Louise Rosenblatt (1978, 1980, 1994, 2002) supports context as a factor in the construction of meaning. She suggests that readers transact with the text and the context in order to comprehend. Transaction implies that readers' personal experiences shape their understanding of narrative (story) and expository (informational) text, indicating that response is personal and may vary. In such a model, the power relationship between the author and the reader shifts somewhat, allowing the reader more authority to read beyond the literal text, but not enough to examine the power relations implied in the text. This kind of interpretation of the text frees the reader from the confines of literal comprehension, because even though the text is written by the author, the comprehension of it is a dialogue between the reader and the author.

Rosenblatt (2002) suggests that stances are "aspects of consciousness." Her Aesthetic-Efferent Continuum (1994) reflects her belief that readers transact with text from aesthetic and efferent stances. The aesthetic stance depicts a more emotional perspective; the efferent stance, a more factual one. Rosenblatt (2002) notes that no reading experience is purely aesthetic or purely efferent, but rather that readers are always making choices about their thinking, focusing on both stances, and sometimes more on one than the other.

The relationship of critical literacy to contemporary beliefs about literacy becomes clear when examining Rosenblatt's work. Reading from a critical stance can be viewed as another component of her continuum. When reading from a critical stance, readers use their background knowledge to understand the power relationships between their ideas and the ideas presented by the author of the text. In this process, readers play the role of text critics (Luke & Freebody, 1999). In other words, readers have the power to envision alternate ways of viewing the author's topic, and they exert that power when they read from a critical stance. The critical stance functions just as the aesthetic and efferent stances do during reading; our reading experiences may involve one stance more than the others, but all three are represented during reading. For example, when reading about the Holocaust, we may respond aesthetically to the poetry and drawings the children created in the concentration camps, efferently to the number of children who died during the Holocaust, and critically to the multiple perspectives through which the Holocaust may be viewed.

Critical Literacy as Action

Critical readers also need to have the courage of their convictions in order to act on their knowledge. For example, after seeing an advertisement for soda and analyzing the advertisement from a critical stance, students might resolve to drink less soda or no soda. They might also begin to speak to others about how such advertisements shape their lives and the lives of friends. This kind of critical literacy goes far beyond what has been understood to be critical thinking, which reflects more "logical thought processes characteristic of the scientific process" (Harris & Hodges, 1995, p. 50). Critical literacy may include but also go far beyond the critical evaluation of texts to look more deeply at the complexities of parts of the text. In critical literacy, readers see beyond the situation to examine it in more complex ways (Wink, 2000).

Reading from a critical stance requires readers to analyze and evaluate texts (books, media, lyrics, hypertext, life relationships), meaningfully question their origin and purpose, and take action by representing alternative perspectives. The goal is for readers to become text critics in everyday life—to comprehend information sources from a critical stance as naturally as they comprehend from the aesthetic and efferent stances.

What Is the Role of Discourse in Critical Literacy?

Discourses are often thought of as conversations, but in critical literacy a discourse is larger than a conversation. A discourse represents the ways reality is perceived and created using language, complex signs, facial gestures, practices (ways of doing things) and pictures, among other things (Leistyna, Woodrum & Sherblom, 1996).

When analyzing discourse in critical literacy it is important to consider the concepts of power, history (or the context in which the discourse occurs), and ideology (Wodak, 2001). Power and ideology are often expressed in hidden ways. Their meaning differs depending on the history or context of the situation. A closer look at each of these three concepts follows. It includes examples from *Smoky Night* by Eve Bunting, a text often read in the primary grades, and *Song of the Trees* by Mildred D. Taylor, a text frequently read in the intermediate grades.

THE CONCEPT OF POWER

As noted earlier, in critical literacy reading is viewed as a power relationship between the author and the readers. This concept refers to power as we know it; it is about authority and control. When readers read texts, it is the authors who have the power to describe situations. It is the authors who have the authority to choose to emphasize certain facts or people and de-emphasize others. As an example of this kind of power, we might think about talking to two children after they have had a fight in the school playground. Each child tries to arrange the facts and people in the story in a way that favors his or her version of the story. Traditionally, in reading, the emphasis has been on the author's—and sometimes the illustrator's—power, but in critical literacy readers who are text critics actively exert their power by questioning the author's and illustrator's messages and their hidden implications.

Primary Level Example of the Concept of Power: Eve Bunting, the author of *Smoky Night*, and David Diaz, the illustrator, emphasize the aspects of the book that reinforce the themes of racial harmony and working together for peace. The book takes place during the 1994 Los Angeles riots. An African-American mother and her son do not like a Korean-American family that owns a neighborhood grocery store. Because of the fires and robberies that occur during the riots, both the African-American family and the Korean-American family eventually find themselves together at a shelter longing for their cats, who are lost. The colors and the objects that the illustrator chooses to use in the paintings are an exercise of his power to depict the scenes in a particular and biased way.

At the beginning, the riots are reflected in the illustrations by the dark purples, grays, and browns that punctuate this terrible event with darkness and malevolence. Orange, yellow, and red, the colors of fires and emergencies, create a sense of tension and urgency in the mind of the viewer. The broken glass, scattered trash, and litter depicted on the border of each of the beginning pages add to the viewer's feeling of disorder and brokenness in the riot. At the end of the book, when racial harmony emerges and the fear of the riot subsides, the illustrations reflect a different mood. The colors become lighter, removing the mystery of darkness, and floral wallpaper appears on the borders to give the pages a more uplifting mood.

When the story begins, David Diaz uses his power as an illustrator to choose certain colors that emphasize the discord of the riot and the friction between the two families. At the end of the story, Diaz exercises that same power to use muted colors and place the characters next to each other in order to emphasize the racial harmony. In this case, the illustrator has power because he chose the colors and the border designs, while the readers/viewers are powerless and must accept the illustrator's choices. With no color or detail, or perhaps with no picture at all, readers might have more power to imagine a scene that draws on their background knowledge. They might imagine more forbidding or even friendlier surroundings.

Upper Grade Example of the Concept of Power: *Song of the Trees* by Mildred D. Taylor, a story that takes place in Mississippi during the Great Depression, is about how the Logans, a black family, keep Mr. Anderson, a white man, from forcing them to sell him trees for an artificially low price. In this book, the author, Mildred D. Taylor, describes actions and dialogue of characters that were passed down to her from her grandfather. The descriptions and characters consistently favor the black family, the Logans, and discount the actions of the white characters in the story. The Logans appear to have the positive role of being environmentalists; they play with the trees, hear their songs, and refuse to allow Mr. Anderson, the white man, to chop them down. Papa Logan appears to be a hero who provides impressive, well-placed comments. Mr. Anderson laughs "weakly"(p. 23) and Pa Logan "smiles cunningly" (p. 50). Even the Logan children, for all their feistiness, are made to seem obedient to their parents and heroic in making the lumbermen look bumbling and impotent. Taylor's favoritism does not diminish the importance of her message, and yet it is appropriate, as a critical reader, to recognize that the author exercises power by showing bias toward her own family in this story.

THE CONCEPT OF HISTORY OR CONTEXT

In addition to expressing a power relationship, language is historical and can only be understood with reference to its context (Meyer, 2001). Context includes such elements as when and where the situation is occurring, who is speaking, who is listening, what the participants know, what has happened prior to the situation, and what illustrations or pictures are present (Janks, 1993). Because situated discourse is the idea that words, sentences, pictures, and gestures carry different meanings in different settings or contexts, it is important to examine the language in the context or setting in which it is expressed.

Primary Level Example of the Concept of History or Context: In *Smoky Night*, Eve Bunting has a character, a young African American, tell the reader, "My mama and I don't go in Mrs. Kim's market even though it's close. Mama says it's better if we buy from our own people." And when Mrs. Kim is being robbed, the African-American family pays no attention. The tension between the African-American and Korean-American families is rooted in centuries-old racism. In their neighborhood, African Americans, who have a high unemployment rate, try to support African American–owned businesses so that African Americans can have jobs. The words "our own people" carry extensive historical baggage, conveying racial tensions that can be interpreted in the light of national and local histories.

Upper Grade Example of the Concept of History or Context: When uttered in isolation, the sentence "It would be too bad if David had an accident," gives the impression that the speaker is sympathetic to David and would feel bad if David had an accident. However, in *Song of the Trees*, the statement has a different meaning. In that novel, Mr. Anderson, a white businessman in the south in the 1930s, pressures Ma, a black woman whose husband is David, to sell her trees to him for sixty dollars. When Mr. Anderson says, "It would be too bad if David had an accident," he is threatening to hurt David unless she sells him the trees. This phrase has a particular meaning in the historical context of the novel, when phrases of this type were often used to intimidate blacks. In another example, a kiss—a form of communication (or discourse)—which often has romantic meanings, is used in the movie *The Godfather* as a signal that someone is marked for murder. As these examples demonstrate, when discourse is analyzed, it must be situated and examined in the historical context in which it occurred.

THE CONCEPT OF IDEOLOGY

Ideology is a belief system that is implied with whatever utterance is made. Linguists have brought to our attention that there are subtle ways in which words are chosen and used that cause readers to be sympathetic to the author's position. These choices are situated in the author's world and reflect the writer's ideological biases. Readers who are able to understand the author's biases have a deeper, more critical understanding than readers who merely accept the author's position.

Advocates of critical literacy believe that all texts have bias to some degree. Because texts can tell only one story or a limited range of stories, emphasizing or foregrounding that story makes them biased. Consequently, bias is a normal, unavoidable part of expression. It is the reader's job to understand the bias and decide how to balance it with his or her own knowledge.

Primary Level Example of the Concept of Ideology: In *Smoky Night*, Eve Bunting writes the words that signify the ideology of reconciliation when Gena, a character in the book, says "My name is Gena" by way of introduction to Mrs. Kim and invites Mrs. Kim and her cat to visit. Mrs. Kim says thank you and "we will come." These words carry great meaning for the two families as they reconcile and rise above racial differences to recognize one another as human beings and neighbors. The author then tells us that the cats, belonging to different families, are purring. Bunting demonstrates her ideological bent toward living together in racial harmony through these carefully chosen phrases that demonstrate understanding and reconciliation.

Upper Grade Example of the Concept of Ideology: In *Song of the Trees*, when Mr. Anderson threatens to harm Ma Logan's husband, the ideology of racism is expressed with the belief that whites are better than blacks and that the typical system of justice and equality does not apply. Such an ideology might not be visible to the literal reader, but when readers take a critical stance and consider the ideology, they understand much more about the meaning of the phrase. They read the word for literal meanings, but they read the world to understand at a deeper level.

Gee (1996) observes that readers use particular discourse resources to construct meanings from texts. He also suggests that although the meaning in language is tied to people's experiences and stored in the brain, it is not stored as static organized propositions as schema theory suggests, but rather as dynamic images—a "videotape" that we can edit and re-edit as needed (Gee, 2001).

Discourse Analysis in the Classroom

Allan Luke (2000, pp. 453–454) supports the situated nature of discourse and reports that the influences of critical discourse analysis result in practical classroom focus on the following:

- ◆ **Identifying diverse and multiple voices at work in texts, giving students explicit access to these cultural and historical positions, and discussing whose interests such texts might serve.**

  Example: When reading about the American Revolution, consider how the account of that historical event might be influenced by the author who wrote it, the country in which the text was published, or other factors. Students might take action by creating a text that represents a different perspective on the conflict.

- ◆ **Identifying the dominant cultural discourses—themes, ideologies, registers—in texts and discussing how these discourses attempt to position and construct readers, their understandings and repre-sentations of the world, their social relations, and their identities.**

  Example: When reading about famous inventors and other people of importance more than a century ago, consider which gender and race were represented and which weren't, and how that influenced people's thinking then and how it affects people's thinking today. Students might take action by researching the contributions of various ethnicities.

◆ **Multiple possible readings of texts, focusing on which ideas, themes, characterizations, and possible readers are silent or marginalized.**

Example: Consider reading a classic novel or popular children's book multiple times to critically analyze the author's message and the choices he/she made regarding character and gender emphasis. To take action, students might write an alternative text emphasizing another gender or different characters.

◆ **Identifying the social relations and sources of power and authority of the institutions (e.g., mass media, workplaces, corporations, governments, educational institutions) where particular texts are used.**

Example: Consider a situation, such as Eastern European countries that were dominated by Communism for 30 years and in which teachers and students were allowed to use only government-authored texts characterized by the absence of critical thinking. Readers might take action by suggesting or creating alternative texts.

◆ **Critique, problem solve, and produce a broad range of texts —traditional and contemporary, canonical and popular, aesthetic and functional—from a range of cultures and institutions.**

Example: Consider reading several cultures' versions of a classic children's story and analyzing each culture's emphasis. Readers might take action by creating their own version of the story.

Allan Luke's practical insights into the situated nature of discourse help us, as teachers, to understand how discourse functions within the context of our teaching. Luke's ideas also provide direction for our planning as we begin to teach from a critical perspective. In the next section, we examine how critical literacy fits within the larger context of school curriculums.

How Does Critical Literacy Fit Into School Curriculums?

In the context of recent developments in education (such as the acknowledgment of sociocultural influences, inquiry-based learning, and attention to the credibility of texts), we might think that reading from a critical stance would have already become a natural part of teaching and learning. But the opposite appears to be true. For many educators, critical literacy seems to be just a theory that has a daunting lexicon. It appears to be veiled in a cloud of mystery—with no connection to practical implementation.

Our goal in writing this book is to demystify critical literacy—to make it accessible for teachers who want to become critically aware and help their students read with deeper understanding. Our task is more involved than writing about traditional reading instruction because there is no single, sure-fire method for reading from a critical stance. That's because critical literacy is a way of thinking—a way of being that challenges texts and life as we know it. As noted earlier in this chapter, critical literacy encourages readers to be active participants in the reading process: to question, to dispute, to examine power relations (Freire, 1970). Consequently, critical literacy is more complex than the traditional reading of a text, which is often accompanied by summarizing what has been read.

When thinking about how critical literacy fits into school curriculums, a number of connections emerge, including:

- national standards
- state standards
- subject areas
- grade levels
- situated, social learning
- multiple modes of expression
- multiple types of text
- technology integration

A discussion of each of these points follows.

National Standards

Our *Standards for the English Language Arts* were developed jointly by the National Council of Teachers of English and the International Reading Association in 1996. (A list of the twelve standards and other excerpts from that document are available on the IRA website at http://www.reading.org/advocacy/elastandards/standards.html.) Standard 11 directly addresses the need for students to be able to participate as knowledgeable, reflective, creative, and critical members of a variety of literacy communities. Other standards address a variety of ideas and conditions that support critical literacy, including that students should be able to:

- ◆ read a wide variety of print and nonprint texts for a variety of purposes including understanding texts, themselves, and cultures; acquiring new information; responding to the needs and demands of society and the workplace; and for personal fulfillment;

- ◆ create, critique, and discuss print and nonprint text;

- ◆ research by generating ideas and questions and posing problems; and evaluate and synthesize information;

- ◆ use spoken, written, and visual language to accomplish their own purposes (e.g., for learning, enjoyment, persuasion, and the exchange of information).

In Australia, there have been several focused initiatives to promote critical literacy at the national level, including the *Adelaide Declaration on National Goals for Schooling in the Twenty-First Century* (1999). This document specifically notes the importance of social justice. For example, the Preamble states, "Australia's future depends upon each citizen having the necessary knowledge, understanding, skills and values for a productive and rewarding life in an educated, just and open society. High quality schooling is central to achieving this vision." The *Adelaide Declaration* further notes that students, when they leave school, should "have the capacity to exercise judgment and responsibility in matters of morality, ethics and social justice, and the capacity to make sense of their world, to think about how things got to be the way they are, to make rational and informed decisions about their own lives and to accept responsibility for their own actions." This is followed by a section in which it is noted that "schooling should be socially just," so that, among other things:

- students' outcomes from schooling are free from the effects of negative forms of discrimination and of differences arising from students' socioeconomic background or geographic location;

- the learning outcomes of educationally disadvantaged students improve and, over time, match those of other students;

- all students understand and acknowledge the value of cultural and linguistic diversity, and possess the knowledge, skills and understanding to contribute to, and benefit from, such diversity in the Australian community and internationally.

The discussions of critical literacy at the national level and the inclusion of ideas that support critical literacy in national standards provide a foundation for infusing critical literacy into state standards and school curriculums. In the next section, we examine how Pennsylvania's and California's standards support reading from a critical stance.

State Standards

Most states use the national standards as a resource when thinking about what they want their students to know and be able to do. So, it is common to see language used at the state level that is similar to that used at the national level. For example, in Pennsylvania, although critical literacy is not specifically addressed, reading from a critical stance would support standards 1.3—Reading, analyzing, and interpreting literature and 1.2—Reading critically in the content areas. In California, the Objectives for English Language Content and Social Studies (http://cde.ca.gov) do not specifically list critical literacy as a goal, but again, the analysis common in critical literacy is present in many forms. Reading from a critical stance helps students achieve a variety of state standards because it requires readers to question and critically analyze text.

Subject Areas

Critical literacy spans the curriculum and extends beyond teaching and learning to everyday experiences. Consequently, students can read from a critical stance in all subject areas, including science (e.g., Is cloning fair?) and social studies (e.g., Has America's treatment of Native Americans over the centuries been socially just?). An example from everyday life can be seen when students begin to naturally "read" (critically examine) situations from a critical perspective and demonstrate greater tolerance or understanding of the points of view of the others involved.

Grade Levels

In school, readers at all grade levels can engage in critical literacy. Of course, students of a younger age benefit from more explanation and demonstration in more scaffolded learning experiences. In *Getting Beyond "I Like the Book,"* Vivian Vasquez (2003) describes powerful critical literacy examples in which kindergarten students have taken an active role. Furthermore, numerous examples of students engaging in critical literacy in the primary, intermediate, and middle school grades are included in Part Two of this volume.

Situated, Social Learning

As noted in the principles of critical literacy, techniques that promote critical literacy are dynamic and adapt to the contexts in which they are used. So, even though there are starting points or strategies that help us to read from a critical perspective, their applications change with the contexts in which they are used.

Multiple Modes of Expression

When responding from a critical perspective, we encourage students to express their ideas in a variety of ways: discussion, sketching, dramatizing, singing, and so on. This not only helps to accommodate students' learning styles but also helps students understand that photographs, paintings, and performances can be viewed from a critical stance.

Multiple Types of Text

When engaging in critical literacy, "text" has a variety of meanings. It may refer to trade books, informational articles, song lyrics, movies, television shows, everyday situations, and more. The term is so far-reaching because reading from a critical stance permeates every aspect of life. (Appendix B provides an extensive, annotated list of books to use when teaching critical literacy.)

Technology Integration

There are many ways in which technology and critical literacy intertwine, but chief among them is using the Internet as an information source. In addition to providing access to numerous, quality websites that provide meaningful informational text, the Internet also helps students understand that the act of challenging texts and authors extends beyond books and magazines to websites. (See Appendix C for annotated examples of theme-based websites.) Computers also offer a range of opportunities to represent new perspectives through the writing of plays and stories and the design and creation of brochures, newsletters, posters, and full-motion multimedia.

How Can We, As Teachers, Become Critically Literate?

Before we can teach our students to become critically literate, we must become critically literate ourselves. This means that when we read, we must move beyond comprehension as we have known it to a new, deeper level of critical understanding.

It is important to note that this doesn't just happen—we cannot just "become" critically literate. It is a process that involves learning, understanding, and changing over time. This includes developing theoretical, research, and pedagogical repertoires, changing with time and circumstance, engaging in self-critical practices, and remaining open to possibilities (Comber, 2001).

Final Thoughts

The information presented in this chapter provides a foundation for our understanding. The principles and dimensions of critical literacy provide insight into what critical literacy is and how it functions. It is a dynamic process that examines power relationships, acknowledges that all texts are biased, and encourages readers to explore alternative perspectives and take action. It expands our thinking and enlightens our perceptions as we read both the word and the world from a critical stance.

The information in Chapter 2 provides a number of starting points to help us further our understanding of critical awareness. In it, we transition from theory to practice by discussing how to teach critical literacy. Instructional frameworks, critical literacy strategies, and texts are among the topics discussed.

Teaching Critical Literacy

"It has taken some time, but my students have learned to comprehend in a deeper way. It's like when we talk about reading beyond, under, over, and around the text. When my students are engaged from a critical perspective, they comprehend beyond, under, over and around their previous level of understanding."

BETH GRESS, third grade teacher

Jennifer is a member of our teacher group. As an advocate of critical literacy, she knows, as we do, that knowledge is socially constructed, open-ended, and continuously unfolding. We also know that critical literacy is acquired over time through thoughtful deliberation and practice. Consequently, it is important that we be patient, thoughtful risk-takers as we strive to create classroom atmospheres that encourage and challenge students to become critically literate.

As teachers, we know that motivation is essential for successful teaching and learning experiences. We want our students to be enthusiastically involved in their learning, so we strive to use engaging texts and teaching techniques. We also know that using instructional frameworks helps us to successfully organize, plan, and teach meaningful lessons.

In this chapter we focus on these and other aspects of teaching critical literacy. We begin by discussing the engaged learner and describing some motivational practices. Next, we present two instructional frameworks, one that we use to teach critical literacy strategies, and another that we use to teach critical literacy lessons in which students apply the strategies. These are followed by descriptions of critical literacy strategies and their classroom applications. Finally, we discuss how to select texts to use when teaching critical literacy and provide some examples.

How Can We Motivate Students to Become Critically Literate?

As with all aspects of learning, engagement and motivation are key factors when teaching critical literacy. We want our students to choose to be actively engaged and to construct personal meaning. Engaged learners are characterized as:

◆ achieving because they want to understand

◆ possessing intrinsic motivations for interacting with text

◆ viewing reading as a thinking process

◆ sharing knowledge through discussion with teachers and peers

◆ reading for different purposes

◆ utilizing background knowledge, and socially constructing meaning

(Guthrie & Wigfield, 1997; Baker & Wigfield, 1999)

As teachers, we can nurture engagement by encouraging students to read for authentic purposes, make personal connections, focus on comprehension, and respond in meaningful ways.

To foster student motivation, we should be good reading models, create book-rich environments, provide opportunities for choice, promote familiarity with books in various genres, and offer incentives that reflect the values of reading (Gambrell 1996). Gambrell, Palmer, Codling, and Mazzoni (1996) note that highly motivated readers read for a wide variety of reasons including curiosity, involvement, social interchange, and emotional satisfaction.

There is a wide variety of ideas and conditions that motivate students to read. We may already be using some of these ideas in our teaching; others may be new. They include but are not limited to:

- Making reading, writing, speaking, listening, and viewing pleasurable, and providing sufficient time for students to engage in these activities.

- Creating a classroom library that includes multiple levels of narrative and informational texts, addresses a wide range of interests, provides access to a variety of genres, and promotes critical analysis.

- Providing time for active, creative responses to texts using discussion and multiple modes of response (writing, sketching, dramatizing, singing, projects, and so on) to promote critical analysis and creation of a range of new literacies.

- Encouraging and valuing students' independent thinking as they read, write, speak, listen, and view.

Although this list contains a variety of ideas, it is not exhaustive. As you prepare to teach your students about critical literacy, we invite you to think about other aspects of your teaching that may contribute to your students' motivation.

What Instructional Frameworks Can We Use to Teach About Critical Literacy?

When teaching students about critical literacy, there are two instructional frameworks we find helpful. The first is used to teach the critical literacy strategies. The second is used to teach critical literacy lessons in which students apply the strategies after they have learned what they are and how to use them. An extensive list of critical literacy strategies and ideas for classroom implementation follows the frameworks.

THE STRATEGY INSTRUCTIONAL FRAMEWORK

When teaching critical literacy strategies, we often use the Guided Comprehension 5-step direct instruction process (McLaughlin & Allen, 2002a). This whole-class process involves explaining, demonstrating, guiding, practicing, and reflecting. In Figure 1, this teacher-directed, scaffolded process is adapted for use in teaching critical literacy strategies.

It's important to note that the teacher reads aloud in each step of this process. The students focus on learning what the strategy is and how to apply it in scaffolded settings. Figure 2 presents an example of using the Strategy Instruction Framework and Seymour Simon's informational book *Wolves* to teach Problem Posing.

THE GUIDED COMPREHENSION DIRECT INSTRUCTION FRAMEWORK

(McLaughlin & Allen, 2002a)

EXPLAIN what the critical literacy strategy is and how it works.

DEMONSTRATE the strategy, using a think-aloud, a read-aloud, and an overhead projector or chalkboard.

GUIDE the students to work in small groups or with partners to create responses.

PRACTICE by having students work with partners or independently to apply the critical literacy strategy.

REFLECT on how the strategy helps students read from a critical stance.

CRITICAL LITERACY LESSON FRAMEWORK

When the students are comfortable using one or more critical literacy strategies, we organize our lessons using the literacy lesson framework presented in Figure 3, which emphasizes engaging, guiding, and extending students' thinking. The format also includes a reflective component. Figures 4, 5, 6, and 7 describe the teaching ideas referenced in the "guiding" segment of the Critical Literacy Lesson Framework: Bookmark Technique, Patterned Partner Reading, Connection Stems, and Say Something. Primary, intermediate, and middle school examples of teacher-authored, classroom-taught lessons based on the Critical Literacy Lesson Framework can be found in Chapters 3, 4, and 5.

What Strategies Can We Use to Teach Critical Literacy?

Critical literacy strategies—or starting points for teaching and learning— help readers to think about texts from a critical perspective. The strategies, which are dynamic and adapt to the contexts in which they are used, promote critical discussions based on reflection and resulting action that leads to more reflection and other resulting actions. Examples of how this works in primary, intermediate, and middle school classrooms can be found in the students' responses in the themed lessons in Chapters 3, 4, and 5.

The purpose of the strategies is to provide direction for students as they engage in critical analysis—examining social issues and power relations. Their role in critical literacy is similar to that of reading comprehension strategies that support students' understanding of text.

In the following section we describe a variety of frequently used critical literacy strategies and provide examples of each. Primary, intermediate, and middle school lessons based on these strategies can be found in Chapters 3, 4, and 5.

FIGURE 2

TEACHING A CRITICAL LITERACY STRATEGY USING THE GUIDED COMPREHENSION DIRECT INSTRUCTION PROCESS

(McLaughlin & Allen, 2002b)

EXPLAIN what the critical literacy strategy is and how it works.

I began by explaining the critical literacy strategy Alternative Perspectives. I explained to students that when we examine alternative perspectives, we explore the points of view of different characters in a story or different people in a real-life situation. I told them that sometimes there are many characters in a book, but the story is usually only told from one character's point of view. I also explained that sometimes factual information is written from just one perspective and that we need to question what that perspective is and what other perspectives might be. I explained that after we read the text, we would discuss it from alternative perspectives and think about what we would do as a result of our reading from a critical perspective.

DEMONSTRATE the strategy, using a think-aloud, a read-aloud, and an overhead projector or chalkboard.

I demonstrated Alternative Perspectives by introducing an informational text, *Wolves* by Seymour Simon. I shared the cover and the title with the students and I read aloud the first few pages of the book. Then I stopped to think aloud about the perspective from which this book was written. I told the class, "As I looked at the cover and started reading, I remembered that a lot of what I know about wolves came from reading fairy tales and stories, and I think the author wants me to have more information about real wolves

because the pictures he includes are pictures of real wolves. I remember that in the fairy tales, the wolves sometimes had kind of sly smiles when they were trying to trick somebody. I also remember seeing some funny drawings of wolves, and wolves that stood up like people, which I don't see in this book by Seymour Simon. In this book there are photographs of real wolves. I wonder if Seymour Simon took the photographs."
I continued to read aloud and think aloud as I finished reading the next segment of the text. I said, "In this book the author says that what we read about wolves in fairy tales is different from the way wolves really are. He shares information, including the fact that a lot of people think about wolves as killers, but a healthy wolf has never killed a person. That's interesting because in the fairy tales I have read, wolves did kill people. So, this has taught me something about how the wolves in fairy tales are different from the wolves discussed in this book."

GUIDE the students to work in small groups or with partners to create responses.

I invited the students to work in small groups and prompted them to consider the perspective from which Seymour Simon had written his book, as I continued to read the text aloud and share the photographs that illustrate it. After providing time for group discussions and monitoring their progress, I asked students to share their ideas with the class. Melissa and David said that they

FIGURE 2 cont.

thought the author wrote from the point of view of someone who knew a lot about wolves, and they wanted to see how many facts they could learn about wolves from this book. Jimez said that he had been in the woods camping, but he had never seen a wolf, so Seymour Simon must know right where to look for wolves. Jimez also wondered if Seymour Simon had to take a lot of pictures and how close he had to get to the wolves to take the pictures. He thought Seymour Simon must really like wolves. Melanie, Jimez's partner, said that the wolves were like us in some ways. She said that they have homes and families and the dad goes out to get food. That makes the wolves seem to be like us. She also said that in the fairy tales the wolves are tricky and mean. Whoever wrote the fairy tales must not have liked wolves. They thought the author wanted us to believe that what he wrote about wolves was the way they really were so that he could encourage people to like wolves and have more wolves in the forest. That led to a discussion of how we could know that what Seymour Simon wrote about wolves was true. We decided that the best way to know that was to check other informational sources about wolves.

PRACTICE by having students work with partners or independently to apply the critical literacy strategy.

The students continued to analyze the perspective represented in the text, and I continued to monitor their small-group discussions. In our subsequent whole-class discussion, Cody said, "Most of what I knew about wolves, I knew from fairy tales. I thought they were scary—like the wolf in *Little Red Riding Hood*. There's a lot more about real wolves in this book. What Seymour Simon said about wolves was different from what I thought about wolves. He saw them in a different way." Cody's final comment launched us into a discussion about the fact that different people can view things in different ways, and we need to think about other perspectives, or points of view, when we are using Alternative Perspectives. Later in our discussion, we decided to make posters that contained drawings and facts about wolves and hang them in the school hallway so that others could learn what we had learned about wolves.

REFLECT on how the strategy helps us read from a critical stance.

After our discussion about *Wolves* ended, we talked about using Alternative Perspectives with other texts in other situations. Alicia said that she thought we could use it when we read stories. So we talked about how we might apply it in *Cinderella*, a story we all knew. The students suggested that the story represented Cinderella's perspective, and could be examined from the stepmother's and stepsisters' points of view, as well as those of the fairy godmother, the prince, and others.

In our next lesson, I introduced a new text and reviewed Alternative Perspectives, making connections to our lesson on *Wolves* and our discussion of *Cinderella*. I could see that the students were progressing in their understanding of how to use this strategy. After using Alternative Perspectives in several more practice sessions, using both narrative and informational text, I could tell that students were comfortable using it, so I integrated it into our critical literacy lessons.

PROBLEM POSING

Problem Posing is a critical literacy strategy that can be used with narrative and informational text, as well as hypertext, a variety of media, and conversations. After reading the text, viewing the video, or discussing the situation that is going to be analyzed, readers engage in critical literacy by using questions, such as the following, to engage in critical analysis:

- ◆ Who is in the text/picture/ situation? Who is missing?

- ◆ Whose voices are represented? Whose voices are marginalized or discounted?

- ◆ What are the intentions of the author? What does the author want the reader to think?

- ◆ What would an alternative text/picture/situation say?

- ◆ How can the reader use this information to promote equity?

For example, readers could use these questions to deconstruct *The Giving Tree* by Shel Silverstein. This story is about a boy who periodically visits the Giving Tree as he ages. (For many people, *The Giving Tree* symbolizes the boy's mother because it is referred to as "her.") Each time he visits the tree, the tree tries to make him happy offering him her leaves for crowns, her apples to eat, her branches to build a

FIGURE 3

CRITICAL LITERACY LESSON FRAMEWORK

ENGAGING STUDENTS' THINKING
Before reading, engage students in the lesson by activating background knowledge, motivating students by introducing the text, and setting a purpose for reading.

GUIDING STUDENTS' THINKING
During reading, help the students engage with the text by prompting them as they read silently, having them engage in Patterned Partner Reading (McLaughlin & Allen, 2002a) or other methods that promote engagement with text, such as the Bookmark Technique (McLaughlin & Allen, 2002a), Connection Stems (Harvey & Goudvis, 2000), or Say Something (Short, Harste, & Burke, 1996). (See Figures 5, 6, 7, and 8 for descriptions of these teaching techniques.)

EXTENDING STUDENTS' THINKING
After reading, help the students extend their reading from a critical stance by engaging in critical discussions and taking action based on what they have read.

REFLECTION At the conclusion of the lesson, reflect on (a) what you taught, (b) why you taught it, (c) how you think the lesson went, (d) how students reacted to the lessons, (e) what you plan to do to continue teaching from a critical perspective, and (f) what additional observations or comments you may have.

FIGURE 4

PATTERNED PARTNER READING

(McLaughlin & Allen, 2002a)

PURPOSES: Patterned Partner Reading promotes strategic reading and provides a structure for reading interactively with a partner. Students can use Patterned Partner Reading with narrative or expository text.

PROCEDURE:

1. Students select a text and a partner with whom they will read, or the teacher selects the text and assigns partners.

2. Partners determine the amount of text they will each read and which of the following patterns they will use to engage in the reading (or the teacher selects which pattern will be used during a particular lesson).

Patterns include but are not limited to:

Read–Pause–Predict: Partners begin by making predictions based on the cover and title of the book. Next, they take turns reading a page silently or orally. After reading each page, they pause to confirm or revise their predictions and make new predictions about the next page. This process continues throughout the reading.

Read–Pause–Discuss: Partners take turns reading a page silently or orally. After reading each page, they pause. Each asks the other a question about the section of the text just read, to which the other partner responds. This process continues throughout the reading.

Read–Pause–Make Connections: Partners take turns reading a page silently or orally. After reading each page, they pause to make and share Text–Self, Text–Text, or Text–World Connections. When using this pattern, students can use Connection Stems, such as "This reminds me of…," "I remember an experience I had like that," "I remember another book I read about this."

Read–Pause–Sketch: Partners take turns reading a page silently or orally. After reading each page, they pause and each sketches an idea from that page of text. Then the partners share and discuss their drawings. (A blackline master that contains multiple sketching spaces facilitates this process.) This continues throughout the reading.

Read–Pause–Bookmark: Partners take turns reading a page silently or orally, pausing periodically to complete bookmarks noting the most interesting information: something that confused them, a vocabulary word they think the whole class should talk about, or an illustration, graphic, or map that helped them to understand what they read.

Read–Pause–Retell or Read–Pause–Summarize: Partners take turns reading a page silently or orally. After reading each page, they pause and the listening partner retells what happened on that page (narrative text) or summarizes (informational text). This process continues throughout the reading.

3. Students discuss in a whole- or small-group setting the text they have read.

house, and her trunk to build a boat, in which the boy sails far away. Though at the beginning the boy is happy with the tree, he never thanks her or gives anything to her.

After reading the text, the teacher might ask, *Who is in the text/picture/situation? Who is missing?* Students are pretty quick to understand that the book is about a boy and a tree that is a symbol for his mother. When they think about what is missing they notice that the mother has no husband, companions, or outside interests other than the boy. This leaves the impression that the mother is totally devoted to her son, with no purpose in life other than to make the son happy. The boy, in contrast, appears to have a full life away from the tree. Although it may not be significant, the fact that the boy has no siblings reinforces the reader's perception of him as the sole focus of his mother's love and attention.

The next concept is difficult for students of any age to understand at first because people so rarely think about voice and the author's intentions. Some possible ways to ask the question are: *Whose voices are represented? Who is the hero of the book? Who do you love in this book? Whose perspective does the author favor?* The reader is *positioned* (see Appendix A) to feel a combination of warmth and sadness for the mother who happily gives everything to the boy. So the voice represented in this book is apparently the voice of self-sacrificing mothers, who receive scant gratitude or love in return. *Whose voices are marginalized or discounted?* While at first the boy plays

> **FIGURE 5**
>
> # BOOKMARK TECHNIQUE
>
> (McLaughlin & Allen, 2002a)
>
> **PURPOSES:** Bookmark Technique helps students monitor their comprehension and make evaluative judgments about texts. Students can use this technique while reading narrative or expository text.
>
> **PROCEDURE:**
>
> **1.** Students create four bookmarks by folding and cutting an 8.5" x 11" sheet of paper into four equal parts (or you can provide precut blackline masters).
>
> **2.** As students read, they make decisions about and record specific information on each bookmark, including the page and paragraph where their choice is located:
>
> **Bookmark 1:** Write about and/or sketch the part of the text that they find most interesting.
>
> **Bookmark 2:** Write and/or sketch something they find confusing.
>
> **Bookmark 3:** Write a word they think the whole class needs to discuss.
>
> **Bookmark 4:** Choose an illustration, graph, or map that helped them understand what they read.
>
> **3.** After reading, the ideas the students have recorded on the bookmarks are used as a basis for discussion.

FIGURE 6

CONNECTION STEMS

(Adapted from Harvey & Goudvis, 2000)

PURPOSES: Connection Stems are prompts that provide a structure to make connections while reading narrative and informational texts. These prompts help students to monitor their thinking and encourage reflection during reading.

PROCEDURE:

1. Students use Connection Stems, such as those listed below, to make connections as they read a text.

2. Students complete Connection Stems orally, in writing, or by sketching.

3. When sharing their completed Connection Stems, students use text support and personal experiences to explain their connections.

4. Students share the completed stems through discussion or journal responses.

5. Students make connections throughout the reading of the text.

    Examples of Connections Stems:

    ◆ That reminds me of . . .

    ◆ I remember when . . .

    ◆ I have a connection . . .

    ◆ An experience I have had like that . . .

    ◆ I felt like that character when . . .

    ◆ If I were that character, I would . . .

    ◆ I remember another book about this . . .

in the tree and is happy, he eventually becomes an ungrateful consumer of his mother's generosity. The boy is not a very admirable character and so his voice is marginalized. Typically, when students realize how they have been positioned by the author, they start to tell stories about how they are not like the boy in the story. They claim that they are helpful to their parents and happy and grateful for the things they are given.

What does the author want the reader to think? This question helps us understand that the author probably has a subtext or a philosophy of life he is forwarding with this book. The reader may conclude that Shel Silverstein's motivation for writing *The Giving Tree* was to promote selflessness and the joy of giving. However, we could also assume that he wanted to protest the inequity in some parent-child relationships.

What would an alternative text/picture/ situation say? The idea here is to get the reader to understand the perspective of the book being analyzed by trying to come up with a story that has an alternative theme or character. In response to this question, some students might imagine a story similar to *The Giving Tree*, except that the child is grateful, or that instead of the parent giving, the child cares for the parent, who may be old or in the hospital. A second example of an alternative text might be a situation in which the boy helps the parent do chores such as washing the dishes and preparing the food. In a third possible alternative text, the mother and the boy both have friends they enjoy and don't appear to be desperately joined together. Coming up with a counter or alternative text can be a very useful tool for clarifying what the original text represents.

How can the reader use this information to promote equity? This question encourages the reader to use the information they learned to promote fairness. In the case of *The Giving Tree*, the reader might reflect on the fact that people sometimes write stories in order to make a point or promote certain standards of behavior. Perhaps such a story establishes high moral ground for the mother, giving her higher status. By paying attention to the motivations of the person who chooses the story or tells the story of *The Giving Tree*, the reader can learn not to be unfairly positioned by another.

FIGURE 7

SAY SOMETHING

(Short, Harste, & Burke, 1996)

PURPOSES: Say Something helps students to monitor their reading by making connections.

Students can use this technique while reading narrative or informational text.

PROCEDURE:

1. Students work in pairs to read a text (student- or teacher-selected).

2. At student-selected or teacher-designated points, students stop to "say something" to their partner about what they have read. For example, what they say might be an idea that was new to them or a comment about a character's actions. (If the text has subheadings, these make good stopping points).

3. Students repeat this process throughout the reading of the text.

In another example, we could use some of these or similar questions to critically analyze a passage in *Harry Potter and the Sorcerer's Stone*. The teacher might ask *Who is in the text and who is missing?* when Hagrid the Giant visits Harry on his birthday to tell him that he will be going to the Hogwarts School of Witchcraft and Wizardry. Hagrid embarrasses Harry's caretakers, the Dursleys, and their son, Dudley, by frustrating and intimidating them. We are led to believe that Hagrid's behavior is justified because Harry has been treated unfairly by his guardian. Readers take joy in seeing Uncle Vernon put in his place by Hagrid, in part because the text seems to favor Harry's perspective and the idea that Harry should exact retribution for the Dursleys' poor treatment of him. Students might observe that the Dursleys' perspective is missing in this passage.

Another perspective that is missing is the idea that instead of mocking the Dursleys, Harry and Hagrid could be more gracious and forgiving toward the Dursleys.

Next, the teacher might question, *What might an alternative text show?* An alternative text might show a polite but persistent Hagrid and Harry helping Uncle Vernon understand the importance of Harry's birthday and impending trip to Hogwarts.

After discussing these points, readers might question, *How can we use this information to promote justice and equity?* Readers need to understand that although most people *enjoy* seeing the pretentious, controlling authoritarian get his due, in reality it is unlikely that a giant (or some kind of superhero) would come to the rescue. The text doesn't inform the readers very well about how to negotiate with bullies such as Uncle Vernon. It tells the readers that even if they think it is wrong, they may enjoy identifying a bad guy in the story and seeing him embarrassed. This, however, does not make the humiliation right or effective. Humiliation deepens divisions between people and promotes misunderstanding. As Harry discovers, Uncle Vernon's anger and distrust of all things magical increases, perhaps in part due to their humiliation of him. Justice and equity would be better served by less humiliating discussions with Uncle Vernon.

The Rest of the Story (McLaughlin, 2000)

The Rest of the Story is an adaptation of Problem Posing that encourages students to use their background knowledge to examine what is missing or underrepresented in a text and to research that perspective. For example, when pondering what is missing from a history text's account of World War II, some may note that information about the Japanese-American Internment is not included. Students can then use other resources, including the Internet, to learn The Rest of the Story about the Japanese-American Internment. Trade books that would support this investigation include *Baseball Saved Us*, *The Bracelet*, and *So Far From the Sea*. (Annotations of these volumes can be found in Appendix B.) Students might discover facts such as that Japanese-American Internment occurred in the United States, that Japanese Americans gave up life as they knew it and were held in internment camps, and that when World War II ended, many of those interned found that their properties, jobs, and businesses had been taken by non–Japanese Americans. When students complete their research, they present it to the class in a mode of their choosing (picture book, press conference, etc.) and use it as a starting point for critical discussion. This helps students demonstrate an understanding of author and text bias.

Switching

Another effective way to prompt students to use Problem Posing is through Switching. In this strategy, after reading the text, the reader responds to selected questions, such as *What gender is represented in the text?* Then, he imagines an alternative version of the story by switching genders, critically analyzing the author's emphasis on one gender and how the message would change if the other gender were emphasized. For example, gender discrimination becomes obvious when reimagining the story of *Homeless Bird* by Gloria Wheelan, in which Koly, a 13-year-old Indian girl, leaves her family to get married. When her husband dies, she cannot remarry or work because of Indian customs. The groom's family, with whom she must live, sees her as a burden, consuming the family resources, and she becomes despised by others and herself. If the reader reimagined the story and created a Gender Switch, putting a boy in Koly's place, the main character's problems would disappear because boys in India don't have the same taboos girls do. The reader could also do a Setting Switch, sending Koly to the United Kingdom where she would be expected to stay in school and would later be allowed to remarry.

Examples of Switching include:

GENDER SWITCH If there are mostly boys in the text, switch the characters to mostly girls. How does your thinking about the story change when you replace key characters with people of the opposite gender? In *The Castle in the Attic* by E. Winthrop, how would the story change if William and his friend the knight were both girls?

THEME SWITCH Make up a different story with the opposite theme or a different but closely related theme as a way to look at the story in a different way. If the theme is "peace is good," imagine a story in which "force is good." How does that change the story? How might *Redwall* by B. Jacques change if Matthias were mostly nonviolent instead of violent in defense of Redwall Abbey?

SETTING SWITCH Tell the story in a different setting—time, place, social class. How would it change the story? How might *Esperanza Rising* by Pam Muñoz Ryan be different if Esperanza were going not from Mexico to California but from Canada to Oregon?

BODY-STYLE SWITCH If the main characters are tall, how would the story be different if they were short? If the main characters are big, how would the story change if they were small? If the main characters are athletic, how would the story change if they were not so athletic? How might *The Bad Beginning: A Series of Unfortunate Events, Book One* by Lemony Snicket change if the Baudelaire children were tall and muscular instead of slight and fragile?

CLOTHING SWITCH How would the story change if the characters were dressed differently—preppy, gang, formally, hip-hop?

EMOTION SWITCH Reimagine a story in which the characters have a different emotional tone. If activity and action are prevalent in the text, make up a story in which the characters are more calm and thoughtful. If the characters are always cracking jokes, reimagine the story with serious characters.

ETHNIC/RACE SWITCH What if the characters were given different ethnic or racial characteristics? What if the main character in *Talkin' About Bessie* by N. Grimes were a white woman instead of Bessie Coleman, an African American? How would the story change?

LANGUAGE SWITCH Tell the story using accents, vocabulary, and expressions from a different country, a different section of the country, the "'hood," or the university. Read "The Really Ugly Duckling," Jon Scieszka's transformational fairy tale from *The Stinky Cheese Man and Other Fairly Stupid Tales*, in a style representing the "'hood." How would that change the story?

RELATIONSHIP/ORGANIZATION SWITCH If the main characters are friends, recreate the story with the main characters as family members. If the main characters are part of a large family and their grandmother is living with them, consider how the story would change if it were about a single person living alone, or a single father with his daughter. Imagine a relationship change in Eve Bunting's *Fly Away Home*. How would it change the story?

Thinking critically about what is missing from a text leads to the exploration of related critical queries, including *Why did the author choose not to report certain information? What did the author want us to believe?* and *What can we do to promote a just understanding of this topic?* These inquiries encourage the students to extend their understanding of power relationships and to take action to promote social justice.

ALTERNATIVE PERSPECTIVES

When we examine alternative perspectives, we explore the viewpoints of different characters in a story or different people in a real-life situation. These characters or people may be present in the story or situation, or they may be created or imagined by the reader. The class then discusses the perspectives in a critical conversation. Formats students have used to share perspectives include focus groups, dramatization, poetry, and song lyrics.

There are a number of critical literacy strategies that help readers create Alternative Perspectives. These include Alternative Texts, Juxtapositioning, Mind and Alternative Mind Portraits, and Theme-Based Focus Groups.

Alternative Texts

An alternative text represents a perspective that is different from the one the reader is reading. When creating an alternative text, the reader perceives the text in a different way and begins to understand the complexity of the issue examined. Alternative texts can be developed when reading narrative or informational text. For example, when reading the traditional story of the three little pigs, students can write an alternative version to develop the story from a different perspective. When reading an informational text, such as P. Busby's *First to Fly*, which recounts the Wright brothers' flying experiences, students could write an alternative historical account told from the perspectives of others who were attempting to be the first to fly a plane. The text can consist of oral, written, visual, or imagined representations including, but not limited to, drawings, oral descriptions, dramatizations, and songs. When using this technique, students can examine the message conveyed by a text, photo, or song and then write an alternative text, take or find an alternative photo, or create counter-lyrics. For example, after seeing a billboard of happy people having dinner in their expensive house, a student might choose to write an alternative text about a family that is sad because it is homeless and depends on shelters for food and beds.

Students can create alternative texts in all subject areas. For example, middle school students created alternative texts in science class after reading newspaper articles about the effects of medical waste pollution on the ocean and about developments in the use of cloning. In music class, the students created alternative lyrics to a variety of songs, including "Cats in the Cradle," and in social studies, they created alternative texts expressing views on a variety of political issues.

CHARACTER SUBSTITUTIONS In this approach, the reader replaces an existing character with a new character that has a different personality. For example, students might substitute their mother, Batman, Sponge Bob, a youth-group leader, or the Cat in the Hat for an existing character and explain what the character would say or do if he/she were in the story. Or, imagine the story of *Cinderella* if Sponge Bob were the prince. Character Substitutions allow students to use their own prior knowledge of different personalities to create alternative texts. In a similar way, students might substitute a different setting for the one in the text.

CHARACTER PERSPECTIVES In this approach, the reader examines the motives of different characters and reorients the facts of the story to fit the desires of one character. In Yangsook Choi's *The Name Jar*, a Korean student, Unhei, is embarrassed when students on the school bus make fun of her name. If Character Perspectives were used with this book, an American student living in Korea might be the character experiencing the embarrassment and sadness caused by the children laughing at her name. As a result of this new perspective, an American reader might better understand Unhei's feelings and have empathy for her.

When there aren't many characters in the story, the reader can construct alternative texts by imagining all of the people that the principal character might be in contact with every day in the community. Then, the reader can describe how the other people in the community might tell the story in a completely different way than does the principal character.

Juxtapositioning

Juxtaposing involves examining two contrasting texts or two pictures next to each other to make the contrast between them obvious. It is used as a strategy to help the reader disrupt the commonplace and see the text in a different way. Readers can also juxtapose different pictures, poems, or songs. This strategy helps the students understand that the same occurrence can be perceived in many different ways and that the story or photo we see in the newspaper simply represents one person's perception of a situation.

JUXTAPOSITIONING TEXTS (McLaughlin & DeVoogd, 2004) When using this strategy, students examine two texts that have been written about the same topic in order to analyze author bias. For example, two editorials—one supporting increased security in schools, one opposing it; one supporting gun control, one opposing it; one supporting a mandatory helmet law, one opposing it—would clearly show how two different writers view a topic. Of course, texts in which the differences in thinking are more subtle can also be used. When a text or situation is described from one point of view only, it is more difficult to discern the bias in the text. However, when readers can compare and contrast the juxtaposed texts, it is easier to see the bias.

PHOTO JUXTAPOSITIONING (McLaughlin & DeVoogd, 2004) When using photo juxtapositioning, two photos that demonstrate different views are examined from a critical stance. For example, Michael Gress, a middle school teacher, juxtaposed two photographs that appeared on the front page of two different American newspapers before the United States went to war in Afghanistan. One photo showed a seven-year-old boy staring into the camera, raising a pistol in the air while sitting on a man's shoulders. Around them, masses of traditionally dressed men with beards held up posters attacking Israel and the United States. The caption on the photo read, "Social Chaos in Afghanistan." The other photo showed a six-year-old Afghani boy running away, carrying his one-year-old sister on his back and looking back over his shoulder in fear. By examining both pictures and discussing them from a critical stance, students came to understand that the photos were not neutral, but rather that each had a strong bias and power to influence the viewer's understanding of which group was the subordinated one. The photographers created the perspectives that were represented.

Mind and Alternative Mind Portraits (McLaughlin & Allen, 2002b)

In this technique (see examples in Chapters 3 and 5) readers examine two points of view. Both may be represented in the story or one may appear in the text and the other silenced or missing from the text. Students begin by selecting the two perspectives they will analyze. Next, they sketch the silhouettes of two heads. In the first silhouette, they write words, sketch drawings, or create collages that represent the first person's perspective. Then they do the same for the second perspective. The completed Mind and Alternative Mind Portraits are shared with peers and used as the starting point for critical discussion. Examples of this can be seen when first grade students, who are reading the Arthur the Aardvark books by Marc Brown, create a Mind Portrait of Arthur and an Alternative Mind Portrait of his sister, D. W., or when older students read *Speak* by Laurie Halse Anderson and create a Mind Portrait for Melinda and an Alternative Mind Portrait for one of her teachers or classmates. In both examples, the completed Mind and Alternative Mind Portraits would be juxtaposed to provide two perceptions of the same story.

Theme-Based Focus Groups (McLaughlin & DeVoogd, 2004)

Theme-based focus groups help students to investigate bias and critically analyze how authors view events from different points of view. When preparing to use theme-based focus groups, teachers choose a text to read aloud to the class and gather a variety of theme-related texts to make available for small-group reading. The teacher reads aloud every day and the students select a related title to read and discuss in a small-group setting. When the read-aloud text and the small-group texts have been read, students leave their original text-based small groups and reorganize into different small groups—groups in which each member has read a different theme-based text. The newly created small groups (Jigsaw II) then discuss the theme, with students contributing ideas based on the text read. Students then engage in whole-group discussion and often extend their thinking by creating theme-related projects.

When using juxtapositioning in theme-based focus groups about World War II, Judy Burke, a sixth grade teacher, used a whole-class setting to read aloud excerpts from *The Greatest Generation* by Tom Brokaw, a theme-related text that represents the perspective of Allied soldiers. Students then self-selected theme-related books and were organized in small groups based on their choices. The theme-based books represented a variety of other perspectives, including those of German soldiers, victims of the Holocaust, victims of the Japanese-American Internment, citizens of Japan, citizens of Pearl Harbor, and a variety of political leaders including Winston Churchill. After the teacher finished reading aloud, the students read and discussed in their small groups the perspective represented in their books. Next, the groups reorganized (Jigsaw II) so that every new group was composed of students who had read novels that represented different perspectives. Small-group discussions focused on multiple perspectives and juxtaposed views. Students began by describing the people or characters in the books they had read and how those characters perceived World War II. Many students found the number of

perspectives surprising, noting that before they engaged in the theme, they had only thought about World War II from the point of view of the American military. They noted that they had failed to consider not only perspectives such as those of the victims of Japanese-American Internment, but also the perspectives of those working on the home front or of families waiting for the soldiers to return home. An interesting discussion of the media also resulted. It focused on the immediacy of information we experience now as compared to the radio news and handwritten letters that were used to communicate military developments during World War II. After in-depth small-group discussion, the students created visual representations of all the perspectives, and the various viewpoints were discussed in a whole-class setting. (See Appendices B and C for texts and websites related to this theme.)

In a fifth-grade thematic study on immigration, Rich Watkins' students chose to read one of five books about the immigrant experience (*Esperanza Rising*, *A Step from Heaven*, *The Other Side of Truth*, *Habibi*, and *Goodbye, Vietnam*) for their theme-based focus group. The understanding of each of the five different situations—Mexican immigrants in a California labor camp, Korean immigrants who thought of America as "heaven," Nigerians smuggled to London after the murder of a parent, an Arab-American family relocating to Jerusalem, and Vietnamese remembering life in Vietnam during the war—

gave the students a much more complex view of the phenomenon of immigration than they could have had after studying just one book. These different perspectives problematize the idea of immigration.

Reading and discussing these books provides a more realistic view of the immigrants' many difficulties and hard-fought victories. The ensuing discussion also disrupts the commonplace notion of the joys of immigration. As a result of this experience, the class found ways to help immigrant students adjust to their new lives.

Critical literacy strategies such as Problem Posing and Alternative Perspectives—and their numerous adaptations—are adaptable across curriculum areas. They provide opportunities to situate critical literacy in a variety of contexts and encourage teachers and students to view critical literacy as a natural part of learning.

How Can We Select Texts to Support Our Teaching of Critical Literacy?

There are numerous examples of narrative and informational text that we can use when teaching and learning about critical literacy. These titles represent multiple genres and run the gamut from informational texts to traditional and transformational fairy tales.

In this section, we explain how these texts support the four dimensions of critical literacy: disruption of the commonplace, examination of multiple viewpoints, focus on sociopolitical issues, and action steps for social justice (Lewison, Flint, & Van Sluys, 2002). A variety of text examples are provided in each category. In addition, numerous annotated titles can be found in Appendix B and websites about selected themes can be found in Appendix C.

It is important to note that although these books facilitate critical literacy experiences, it is not the reading of these texts that generates critical consciousness but rather the critical analysis and discussion in which we and our students engage. It is our questioning, examining, exploring, probing, and juxtaposing that refines our critical awareness and encourages our students to read from a critical stance.

Books That Disrupt the Commonplace and Provide Multiple Viewpoints

Some books are better at eliciting a critical response because the content or tone causes the reader to view a common situation from an entirely different perspective, disrupting stereotypical and commonly held assumptions. For example, in *A Special Fate: Chiune Sugihara, Hero of the Holocaust* by Alison Leslie Gold, a Japanese diplomat working in Lithuania acts in uncharacteristic ways by signing the transit visas of thousands of Jews throughout Europe, allowing the Jews to escape Nazi persecution during World War II. This text provides an alternative viewpoint to the idea that the Japanese were uncaring during World War II. It problematizes our understanding of what it meant to be Japanese during the war. This book also provides a good example of someone taking action toward promoting social justice.

Other texts present a range of perspectives. For example, *Bull Run* by Paul Fleischman recounts the famous Civil War battle from thirteen different perspectives, including those of a Union general, a slave caring for her master, who is a southern soldier, the sister of a soldier from Minnesota, and a physician. Similarly, *Talkin' About Bessie* (Grimes) presents multiple perspectives on Bessie Coleman's life. Family members, friends, and her flight instructor share their perceptions of the first African-American female pilot. Texts such as these facilitate juxtaposing alternative viewpoints.

Texts can also combine pictures and words in ways that encourage readers to understand the text on several different levels. For example, in *CLICK, CLACK, MOO: Cows That Type* (Cronin), farm animals complain about being cold at night, attempt to negotiate, and finally go on strike to force Farmer Jones to buy them electric blankets. Although at first glance this appears to be a humorous picture book about cows and a farmer, it can also be viewed as a story that recounts the power of organized labor in the negotiation process.

With some books, readers or viewers need to draw upon the different stories told in multiple-sign systems. For example, *Life Doesn't Frighten Me* (1998) is a picture-book treatment of a poem written by Maya Angelou and illustrated by Jean-Michel Basquiat. Angelou's words dance whimsically with the unconcerned voice of an innocent child ("I go boo/Make them shoo/I make fun/Way they run") while Basquiat's pictures have a raw, edgy quality that makes them seem frightening. Based on the pictures alone, one might perceive the story in one way; based on the text alone, one might perceive it very differently.

Transformational fairy tales also disrupt the commonplace and help readers perceive multiple points of view. David Wiesner's book *The Three Pigs* is a good example of this. In this version of the classic fairy tale, the pigs get sneezed off the page of their story and blown into several other classic children's tales. In the end, the pigs decide to return to their own story, bringing with them a dragon from another tale to protect them from the wolf. In addition to the traditional fairy tale text, the pigs speak in different registers, making comments in comic-book speech bubbles such as "Hey! He blew me right out of the story!" Even the dragon's grateful and polite commentary opens up new character and plot possibilities when the dragon thanks the pig for taking him out of the book just as the prince was about to slay him ("Many thanks for rescuing me, O brave and noble swine"). Such shifting of registers is also common in the Magic School Bus series, in which the students in the class not only give information about the topic and participate in the narrative, but also comment, in speech bubbles apart from the story, about how they are feeling and what they are thinking. The use of nontraditional plots, characters, and settings challenges reader expectations and requires different ways of reading and viewing (Smith, 2003).

Some books actually invite the reader to recast the story from a different perspective or to recast it as if the reader were in the text providing multiple viewpoints. For example, throughout *The Cat in the Hat* by Dr. Seuss, the fish reminds us about what mother would think about having the Cat in the Hat in the house. He begs us to think about the story from the mother's perspective. Also, at the end of the book Seuss asks readers whether they would tell the mother what happened that day while she was gone.

Other books are intentionally written in a style so open-ended that the author requires the reader to carry the plot, character, or setting—allowing for multiple meanings in the story (Smith, 2003). In David Macaulay's *Black and White*, the story is separated into four different adjoining illustrated texts, each requiring the reader to construct what is happening in the story and how it relates to the other simultaneously progressing plots and characters. Similarly, in wordless picture books, such as David Wiesner's *Sector 7* and Alexandra Day's series about the dog Carl, it is the reader who determines the perspectives and the story emphases.

Books That Focus on Social or Political Issues Between Individuals or in Society

Books that focus on social or political issues between individuals or in society at large provide rich contexts for discussions about critical literacy. For example, many books about the Holocaust encourage exploration of political and social issues of government and morality. Examples include *Number the Stars, Night,* and *My Hundred Children.*

Letters from Rifka by Karen Hesse offers examples of social and political immigrant issues that provide opportunities for students to take different views on freedom in society, disease control, and difficulties encountered during immigration.

In Ji Li Jiang's *Red Scarf Girl: A Memoir of the Cultural Revolution*, a family wants to follow Mao but suffers many indignities because the grandfather had been a landlord. Political relationships interweave with social relationships in the very repressive society in China.

Books That Focus on Action for Social Justice

There are many biographies and other books that describe actions people have taken to achieve social justice. Readings of these texts generate interesting critical discussions about ways in which people can be powerful in their own worlds. In *Nobody in Particular: One Woman's Fight to Save the Bay* by Molly Bang, Diane Wilson, the main character in this true story, tells how she, a shrimper with no education, negotiates with chemical companies for them to clean up the water. *The Story of Ruby Bridges* by Robert Coles recounts the story of the young girl who was the first black child to attend an all-white school in New Orleans, Louisiana, in 1960. And *Martin's Big Words: The Life of Dr. Martin Luther King, Jr.,* by Doreen Rappaport describes the ways in which things Dr. King learned as a child helped him later in life and how nonviolent protest convinced lawmakers to vote to end segregation in the South. Dr. King's life is also wonderfully recounted in *My Brother Martin: A Sister Remembers Growing Up with the Rev. Dr. Martin Luther King, Jr.,* a picture book written by his sister, Christine King Farris.

These books and numerous others, including those annotated in Appendix B, work especially well for teaching about critical literacy. They demonstrate to readers of all ages that their actions can change the world.

Final Thoughts

Contexts that foster critical literacy are characterized by critically aware teachers, actively engaged students, motivational settings, critical literacy strategies, thought-provoking texts, and substantial amounts of critical discussion. Contexts such as these support our students' introduction to reading both the word and the world—to becoming critically aware.

In Part Two, we contextualize the critical literacy strategies in teacher-designed lessons at various grade levels. The lessons, which explore Challenging the Text, Identities, and Seeing Beyond the Bias, are shared in the teachers' voices and feature numerous examples of student work.

Critical Literacy in Action

I n this section, we focus on classroom applications of critical literacy and teachers' and students' reflections on the process. Chapters 3, 4, and 5 feature theme–based lessons for primary, intermediate, and middle school grades. In Chapter 3, Challenging the Text, the reader takes a skeptical stance, posing questions and wondering how the text might be biased. In Chapter 4, the theme of Exploring Identities analyzes who the characters in the story or people in the informational text are or could be. Chapter 5, Seeing Beyond the Bias, helps readers not only to recognize bias, but also imagine different, possible realities. The theme–based chapters are followed by Chapter 6, Reading a Whole New World, which recounts the teachers' and students' reflections on their work in the beginning stages of critical literacy, and offers our final thoughts.

Challenging the Text

"As I watched a movie about the captains of industry, I wondered why it only recounted the company presidents' perspective. I wondered who had written and produced such a one-sided chronicle of the troubles the rich and famous had with their workers. I wondered why there was no mention of workers organizing to obtain safe conditions and a living wage. Then I remembered reading a news article about clothing produced in sweatshops and vowed never to buy that label again. In the course of my critical reflections I realized I should add *Lyddie* by Katherine Patterson to the list of books my students and I discuss when we study American Industrialization."

TOM FLOWERS, fifth grade teacher

Readers who are critically aware see beyond the literal level of the text. They question in order to understand the author's intent, the way ideas are arranged or emphasized, and the purposes of production. They challenge the text. In the example that opens this chapter, Tom, one of the teachers we've been working with, not only comprehends the text (movie), but he also asks himself who is in the movie and who is missing, who is marginalized or made to look like a striking worker making trouble for the captains of industry. He wonders whether the movie's production and presentation on television were sponsored by present-day industrialists seeking to discredit organized labor. He asks himself how he might use this knowledge for social justice (see Appendix A)—to promote fair pay and healthy working conditions for textile workers—when he shops for clothing. He also wonders how he might help make his students aware of the different ways they could respond to the texts they will be reading in his class.

This chapter focuses on challenging the text to access critical understanding. In this process, once the reader has a literal understanding of the text, he/she then poses questions that could lead to critical understanding. It is important to note that going through the motions of answering questions is not critical literacy; rather, critical literacy involves the reader's understanding of the author's intent, bias, and purpose for writing.

We begin this chapter by discussing how to use Problem Posing to challenge texts and by delineating a variety of questions that underpin the strategy. Next, we share teacher-authored critical literacy lessons that focus on using Problem Posing to challenge the text at the primary, intermediate, and middle school levels. Finally, we reflect on the critical nature of the lessons.

Using Problem Posing to Challenge Text

Inquiry underpins critical literacy. When we read from a critical stance, we use questions to challenge the text—to see past the literal meaning of the text to examine issues such as what the author wants readers to believe, and which gender, ethnic group, or philosophy is focused on in the text and which is missing, discounted, or marginalized.

Problem Posing is a strategy in which the reader uses inquiry to challenge the text, just as Tom did in the opening scenario. And although there is no one question or set of official critical literacy queries, we have found the following questions to be useful when we analyze text from a critical perspective:

◆ Who or what is the focus in the text and whose viewpoint is expressed?

◆ Whose voices are missing, silenced, or discounted?

◆ What does the author want readers to believe?

◆ How might alternative perspectives be represented?

- How would examining alternative perspectives contribute to understanding the text from a critical stance?

- What action might readers take based on what they have learned?

When using Problem Posing, it is often helpful to view these questions in more detailed ways. In Figure 8, we list questions that specifically address gender, ethnicity, and emotions.

These questions make it obvious to the reader that every text, every movie, every situation foregrounds, or gives emphasis to, certain types of people or topics, certain viewpoints, and certain activities, while discounting and silencing others. This idea, which reflects an author's power to communicate his/her beliefs, is one of the important principles of critical literacy. Since there is no one story or text that could represent all of the tensions representative of any issue, most advocates of critical literacy suggest that readers study a range of different stories or perspectives in order to arrive at a complex and sophisticated point of view on the issue.

Because the purpose of Problem Posing is to provoke critical understandings of the text, it is not necessary to slavishly list and answer each question. It is rather a matter of choosing those queries that will facilitate critical understanding. In the next section, we present lessons that demonstrate various ways in which teachers have used Problem Posing at various instructional levels to help students challenge texts.

FIGURE 8

PROBLEM-POSING QUESTIONS

(The teacher may adapt the wording to accommodate students' level of understanding.)

❶ Who or what is in the text?

- What gender is the focus or is viewed as more important in the story? Are the boys or the girls the most important characters in the story? Who does most of the talking? Whose picture is seen?

- What point of view is presented by the characters in the text? Is the winner or the loser telling the story?

- What ethnic group or race is most common?

- What type of family seems normal in the text?

- What setting, country, state, or neighborhood appears to be most common in the text?

- What emotional or physical state seems the best in the text? Does being calm or being active appear to be treated as better in this text?

❷ Who or what is missing from the text?

- What gender is missing? Are boys or girls missing in the story?

- What point of view is lacking? Is the antagonistic person's point of view explored?

- What ethnic group or race is uncommon?

- What type of family seems unusual in the text?

- What race is not present?

- What setting, country, state, or neighborhood is left out of the text?

❸ What is marginalized?

- What gender is marginalized? Does the author favor boys or girls?

- What viewpoint is ridiculed? Who are perceived to be odd because of their beliefs?

- What setting, country, state, or neighborhood do characters scorn? What place do the characters dislike?

- What emotional tenor seems absurd in this text? Does it seem better to be spontaneous or well-organized, giving or withholding, happy or serious? Are people with different, creative ideas thought of as weird, or are they admired in this text?

- Are people with particular body types, hairstyles, cars, clothes, or attitudes admired in this text? What body type, hairstyle, car, clothes, or attitudes might not be admired?

④ What does the author want you to think?

- What message does the text seem to convey?

- What do the "good" characters do that makes them so "good"? The "bad"?

- What are the values we might learn to use in our lives after reading this book?

⑤ What story might an alternative text tell?

GENDER SWITCH If there are mostly boys in the text, create a story in which the characters are mostly girls. How would that change the story?

THEME SWITCH Make up a story with the opposite theme or different but closely related theme as a way of looking at the original theme in a different way. How would this change the story's message?

BODY-STYLE SWITCH

If the main characters are tall, how would the story be different if they were short? If the main characters are big, how would the story change if they were small? If the main characters are athletic, how would the story change if they were not?

CLOTHES SWITCH

How would the story change if the characters were dressed differently—preppy, gangsta rapper-style?

ETHNIC/RACE SWITCH

What if the characters were given different ethnicities or races? How would that change the story?

EMOTION SWITCH Make up a story in which the characters exhibit a different emotional tone. If activity and action are honored in the text, make up a story in which the characters are calm and thoughtful. If cracking jokes seems the best way to be in the text, try reimagining the text with the best characters being serious instead.

RELATIONSHIP/ ORGANIZATION SWITCH

If the main characters are friends, try portraying them as family members. If the main characters are part of a large family and grandmother is living with them, think about a single person living alone or a single father with his child. How do these switches change the story?

SETTING SWITCH

Tell the story in a different setting, country, neighborhood, or social class. Explain how it would be different.

LANGUAGE SWITCH

Tell the story using accents, vocabulary, and expressions from a different country or neighborhood—England, the South, the "'hood."

④ How can information from the text be used to promote justice? (Action steps)

- How will my attitude or actions change about this topic?

- How will I treat others differently as a result of having critically analyzed this topic?

- What could I do to change a rule, a procedure, or an attitude that is unjust? To learn more about it?

For example, could I write a letter or have a conversation?

- How can I support those who are treated unfairly?

Classroom Lessons in Which Readers Challenge the Text

This section features various lessons at the primary, intermediate, and middle school levels, in which readers challenge the text. These lessons focus on Problem Posing and provide insights into teachers helping students to disrupt texts and authors, provide different viewpoints, focus on power relationships between people, and think about how to take action and promote social justice (see Appendix A). The teachers who designed

FIGURE 9

OVERVIEW OF LESSONS IN THE CHALLENGING THE TEXT THEME

LEVEL	TEXT	CHALLENGING THE TEXT CRITICAL FOCUS
Primary	*No, David!*	Who is in the story? Who is missing or marginalized?
Primary	*The Rainbow Fish*	What does the author want readers to believe?
Intermediate	*Number the Stars*	Whose voices are missing? How might they be represented? Mind and Alternative Mind Portraits
Middle School	*The Wretched Stone*	Whose viewpoint is expressed? Whose voices are missing, silenced, or discounted? What does the author want readers to believe? How might alternative perspectives be represented? How would that contribute to understanding the text from a critical stance? What actions might readers take based on what they have learned?

and taught these lessons used the instructional framework described in Chapter 2 that focuses on engaging, guiding, and extending students' thinking. Each of the lessons is described in the teacher's own words, and each includes text summaries and examples of student work. Figure 9 provides an overview of the lessons.

CRITICAL LITERACY LESSON

BOOK: *No, David!*
TEACHER: Denise White
GRADE: 2

TEXT SYNOPSIS David Shannon wrote the story *No, David!*, a Caldecott Award–winning book, for the first time when he was five, and then re-created it as an adult. The book's meaning is communicated through text as well as through the illustrations. The pictures show a normally excited David reaching for cookies and the text reading, "No, David!" and David reaching for the goldfish bowl and the text reading, "No, David!" The book shows David trying to do many different things and the text telling David "No!"

GETTING STARTED In the following lesson Denise White, a second grade teacher who was just beginning to teach critical literacy, describes how she engages, guides, and extends students' critical understanding of the text by posing just a few questions after reading *No, David!* to her class and creating alternative texts. Denise began her lesson on challenging the text by choosing a book the students enjoyed. After reading it, she asked them whose voice (perspective) was represented (who was talking?) and whose voice was missing. Here, voice refers not only to who has dialogue but also whose perspective is represented. Because Denise teaches young children, she adapted the questions we had been using. When working in similar settings, you may wish to use questions such as *Whose side is the author on? Who comes out as the hero in the story and who is the bad guy? Who is being hurt unfairly and who is being mean?*

As you are reading Denise's description of her critical literacy lesson, notice how the students come to understand what voices are missing and what the pictures are showing and not showing. Observe how questions concerning who is talking and who is pictured in the text help the students understand the perspective of the book and how questions concerning what is missing help students construct other possible understandings. Finally, note how Denise adapts her questions slightly so that her students will understand her purpose in asking.

ENGAGING STUDENTS' THINKING To introduce reading from a critical stance to my second grade students, I chose the book *No, David!* by David Shannon for three reasons. First, it was a class favorite. My students asked for this book to be read to them repeatedly and never seemed to tire of the colorful illustrations, the silly antics of the main character, or David's mother always telling him no. Second, I knew my students' ability to make personal connections to the text, comparing it to their own experiences making mistakes and their mothers' reactions. Third, my students never questioned why David does the things he does. They just accepted the fact that he is a troublemaker who never listens to his mother, so it offered students many opportunities to think, question, and analyze David's actions and his mother's responses as a way to understand the author's intent as well as what perspectives are left out.

I began by inviting the class to sit on the carpet in front of me. I showed the book to the students and had them tell me what they remembered about the story. A class discussion ensued. Next, I told the students that I was going to read the story again, but this time I wanted them to think about who was in the story and who was missing. I also wanted them to think about who was doing the talking and whom we never heard from.

FIGURE 10

DENISE'S ADAPTATIONS OF PROBLEM POSING QUESTIONS

Problem Posing Questions	Adaptations for Second Grade
Who is in the text?	Who is doing the talking?
Whose voice is missing?	Who doesn't talk?
Who is telling the story? What do they want you to think?	What do you think David is thinking in this picture?
Who is missing? Who is marginalized?	How come we never see the mom?
What story would an alternative text tell?	What would Mom say if she told the story?

GUIDING STUDENTS' THINKING I read the story to the class and we began our discussion. I initiated the first question that began our group discussion and modified the questions as needed to prompt students' responses (see Figure 10).

What follows is an excerpt from our discussion:

Denise:	Whose voice is missing in the story?
Students:	(No response.)
Denise:	(I thought I should change the words because the students didn't seem to understand the "voice is missing" phrase.)
	Who does all the talking in the story?
Students:	The mom.
	She is mad at David for making a mess.
	David doesn't listen to his mom.
Denise:	Then whose voice is missing in the story? Who doesn't talk?
Students:	David.
	How come we never see the mom?
	Yeah, there's no picture of David's mom.
Denise:	Why didn't the illustrator include a picture of David's mom?
	We don't see the mom and we don't know what David is thinking.
	What do you think David is thinking in this picture? [David is reaching up to a fish bowl high on a shelf he can't quite reach.]
Students:	David wants to help his mom feed the fish.
	He wants to see them better.
	He wants to touch them.
	He wants to kill them and eat them.
Denise:	Very interesting. We hear mom telling David "No!," but we don't know what she is thinking, either, and the author doesn't tell us.
	What do you think his mom is thinking about when she sees David climbing on the chair to get the cookies?
Students:	He never listens to his mom, and she wants him to listen.
	She doesn't want him to make a mess because she will have to clean it up.
	His mom thinks David could hurt himself.
	He could break a bone.
	David should listen to his mom because she still loves him.

Although my class had heard and enjoyed this story many times, it was interesting to see them start to look at the text a little differently and question what was going on in the illustrations. When we began the discussion, it started off slowly, with one or two students giving most of the responses, but as we continued, more students joined in with their ideas. One idea would usually spark another. As a result, the class was able to look at both sides of the story. They became more sympathetic toward David, realizing that maybe he just wants to help his mom or that he is hungry and not necessarily trying to cause trouble. They also sympathized with his mom because David always seems to find trouble and make a mess for her to clean up. By the end of our discussion, the class had considered David's feelings as well as his mother's. They also began to understand that the author may not tell you everything and that you need to read the text carefully to find out what might be missing.

I could see through our discussion that the students were beginning to think critically because they were seeing beyond what was written in the text. They were thinking about different viewpoints other than the one that was explicitly presented in the text. I wanted to extend and reinforce those thoughts by having the students draw a picture. I thought maybe the drawing of the picture and the conversation with me or with other students surrounding the creation of that drawing might encourage students to think even more about the viewpoints that were present in the book and those viewpoints that were missing.

EXTENDING STUDENTS' THINKING After the discussion, students drew pictures with captions to create responses to the questions posed during the reading. Though, as is often the case with beginners, some of the student pages mimicked the original text, there were texts and pictures that reflected important differences in the students' thinking. Some of the texts give voice to David's thoughts and desires. In Figure 11 the text says, "David is going to play baseball in the house. He thinks he is not going to break something, and he did."

Other students created pictures that elaborated on the mom's responses beyond the short-tempered, "No, David!" For example, one student wrote, "David wants the cookies and he can break stuff and his mom will have to clean all the stuff." This tells about the desires of the mother, elaborating on the book and giving voice to a more reasonable mom. In Figure 12, the picture shows David splashing in the bathtub and spilling water on the floor. The text repeats Mom's "No!" but elaborates by stating, "and she does not want the house to sink."

David is going to play baseball in the house. he thinks hes not going to brack Somthinge, and he did.

David is. taking a bath and he splashing to much. MOM thinks No!NO!NO! and She dose not what the house to Sink.

FIGURES 11 & 12

In the final response, we see a picture of Mom, a seemingly normal and pleasant person, stretching out her hands to her son. This picture, seen in Figure 13, tells a different story from the book, in which the mother does not appear. Here, the mother is kind and caring, not domineering and demanding.

REFLECTION It was hard for students to understand what I meant by the question *Whose voice is being heard?* Although the mother is speaking throughout the story, the story itself comes from the perspective of David, who only remembers hearing a stern, "No!" Although the mother talks, the book is written in David's voice because the story is how he remembers it and it reflects his bias.

FIGURE 13

Even though we were just beginning to work on becoming critically literate, it was amazing to see how this book, which we had already read and talked about so many times, began to take on a whole new world of meanings after we learned to use critical questions to challenge the text.

FINAL NOTES ABOUT THE *NO, DAVID!* LESSON It is particularly interesting to note that the students don't appear to understand what Denise is asking when she queries about the "voices" in the text. When she uses the word "talking" instead of the word "voices"—changing to use more familiar language—the students understand and engage from a critical stance.

Students also come to understand, through their responses to the teacher's questions and their alternative understandings of the situation through the pictures, that the author's ideas were not the only possible explanation about what happened in the text but were rather a biased retelling. In their drawings explaining the different possible meanings to the story, the students began to imagine a more complex reality taking place outside the limited views expressed in the book.

BOOK: *The Rainbow Fish*

TEACHER: Cathleen Perez

GRADE: 2

TEXT SYNOPSIS In *The Rainbow Fish* by Marcus Pfister, a fish is shunned by the other fish in the ocean because he won't share his colorful scales. An octopus advises Rainbow Fish to share his scales so that he can have friends. In the end, Rainbow Fish shares his scales with the other fish and he feels happy.

GETTING STARTED Cathleen Perez chose *The Rainbow Fish*, a book with a controversial yet strong moral lesson. After reading the book and recognizing the moral lesson the author wanted students to learn, the teacher challenged the moral lesson by persistently asking if that was always the right thing to do.

Although this type of critical literacy is new to her class, Cathleen wants to see her students not be limited to a literal comprehension of the text, so she engages the students in questions to challenge or disrupt the text and imagine this story from a different viewpoint. When reading this lesson, notice that Cathleen persists in exploring a single question to help students understand the themes of the book from different perspectives.

ENGAGING STUDENTS' THINKING I began my critical literacy lesson by introducing the book I wanted to use to teach my students about Problem Posing. To do so, I adapted the Problem Posing question *What does the book want me to believe?* to the more pointed *Should a person have to give something to another person to make a friend?*

GUIDING STUDENTS' THINKING As I read *The Rainbow Fish*, I believed that my second grade class would think that the book was telling us that it is good to share with your friends. And that was their first response. But after our second reading, we discussed how to make friends, and I asked the class, "Should we have to give something to another person so that he or she will be our friend?"

My question prompted the students to begin to look at the story from a different perspective and engage in a critical discussion that showed the text's bias. David responded by saying that we shouldn't have to buy someone's friendship. He continued, "Why should Rainbow Fish have to give the little fish his scales just so he can have a friend? What if the Rainbow Fish runs out of scales? Will the other fish still want to be friends with him?" David started to think about times that other kids had come up to him and asked for something that he had, such as a snack or a football. The other kids would say, "I'll be your friend if you share." When David refused, the other kids would say he was mean.

Another student, Emily, responded that Rainbow Fish's scales were his own, so why should he have to share them? "They belonged to Rainbow Fish, so why is he mean to say no?" Emily believed that it wasn't right for the other fish to say Rainbow Fish was mean. "What if his mom didn't want him to share? He isn't mean."

Other students followed up David's and Emily's responses with similar statements about how Rainbow Fish wasn't mean, and provided their own examples of kids sharing and not sharing. Finally, our discussion turned to what we would do in our lives (what action we would take) based on the theme of *The Rainbow Fish*. David responded that we could make sure we make friends because we like someone, not because of something they have. I believe David was thinking back to his previous discussion about kids that tell him they will be his friends if he shares something with them. Other students responded that we should be friends with someone because they are fun to play with or because they like to do things we like to do, like playing soccer or coloring. These student responses showed the students not only had understood the text but had also seen beyond the text and its themes to alternative versions of the story.

EXTENDING STUDENTS' THINKING In our next class, we created posters of things that the Rainbow Fish could have said to the other fish when they asked him to share his scales. Most of the students focused on their belief that someone should not have to share just to have friends.

After making the posters, my students dramatized an alternative to Rainbow Fish's encounter with other fish. We used the question, "What would an alternative text tell?" We discussed what Rainbow Fish could have said to the other fish, and what the other fish's responses might have been, such as, "I can't give you my scales, but I'd like to play tag with you." My students worked with partners and each pair pretended to be Rainbow Fish and the Little Blue Fish. My students produced several different responses, including dramatic creations of alternative stories. Figure 14 contains a photo of one of them.

FIGURE 14

REFLECTION My students' scenarios included Rainbow Fish telling the other fish that he was mean for telling him he had to give away one of his scales, and the other fish apologizing and saying he just wanted to be friends; Rainbow Fish telling the other fish that we shouldn't have to give something away just to be friends; and, finally Rainbow Fish asking the other fish, "Why can't you like me just for who I am?" and "Why do I have to share my scales to get them to be my friends?" (See Figures 15 and 16 for sample drawings.) I was pleasantly surprised at how my class's responses got more detailed and thoughtful as our discussion moved on. I attempted to guide them without feeding them responses.

FINAL THOUGHTS ABOUT THE *RAINBOW FISH* LESSON The author leads the reader to a particular understanding of the theme of the book: sharing is a good way to get friends. In her questions, Cathleen challenges the author's theme by asking, "Should a person have to give something to another person to make a friend?" She disrupts the students' commonplace understanding of the text, seeking to examine the ideas in more depth and complexity. Applying these thoughts to their own lives, students start to question the author's intent, offering an alternative viewpoint. The impression given from the student comments referring to the exchange of friendship for gifts shows that students are beginning to understand not only the power relations between people but also how they will take critical action in their own lives when something such as friendship is expected in exchange for gifts.

FIGURES 15 & 16

BOOK: *Number the Stars*

TEACHER: Amy Homeyer

GRADE: 5

TEXT SYNOPSIS In this novel by Lois Lowry, a ten-year-old Danish girl named Annemarie and her family risk their own safety to help Annemarie's best friend and her Jewish family escape to Sweden where they will be safe from the Nazis.

GETTING STARTED Amy was just beginning to teach critical literacy, but she thought that the Holocaust, the theme her class was studying, would be a good one for introducing reading from a critical stance to her students. After selecting *Number the Stars* as the focus text, the students and Amy discussed their connections to and background knowledge of World War II and the Holocaust. This gave the students a sense of ownership over the topic. In order to get students to see beyond the text to different viewpoints, she then asked critical questions about *The Diary of Anne Frank*, a book they were already familiar with. She asked, "Whose voices are missing?" and "How might alternative perspectives be represented?" After becoming familiar with asking and answering these and other critical questions, students started reading *Number the Stars*. At various points in the reading, Amy and her students engaged in critical response discussions.

ENGAGING STUDENTS' THINKING Before beginning to read the book, I wanted to engage the students in the themes common in *Number the Stars* so that student discussions would not be so tightly tied to the book but rather to the themes in the book. Our first step was to make connections to World War II and the Holocaust. I began the lesson by introducing the Holocaust through a semantic map (see Figure 17). When the map of background information was completed, we made connections to some of the terms it contained, including World War II. For example, Maria said, "My grandfather was in that war." José said, "I saw a movie about that war. We won that war." When we talked about concentration camps, Caleb said, "I know that Jewish people were kept there against their will." Shaneka said, "There were children in some of those camps." When we talked about the Holocaust Museum, George said, "It's in Washington, D.C." Rosaria said, "I've been there, too. I saw

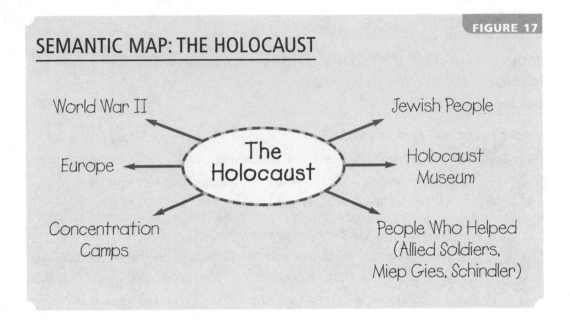

FIGURE 17

SEMANTIC MAP: THE HOLOCAUST

World War II

Jewish People

Europe

The Holocaust

Holocaust Museum

Concentration Camps

People Who Helped (Allied Soldiers, Miep Gies, Schindler)

David's room when I went there." Finally, we used the semantic map and the connections we made as the basis of an extended discussion about the Holocaust. Students also accessed information from several websites at this point. For a listing of these sites, including brief descriptions and website addresses, see "World War II" in Appendix C.

GUIDING STUDENTS' THINKING Next, I introduced *Number the Stars* and explained that we would be reading to find out whose voice was left out of the story and in what ways the story was biased towards particular characters. I introduced Problem Posing and explained that we would be using it to challenge the early chapters of the novel. I explained that we would be focusing on two questions:

◆ Whose voices are missing, silenced, or discounted?

◆ How might alternative perspectives be represented?

In order to demonstrate the use of the critical questions, I used the ideas in the book *The Diary of Anne Frank*. Then we discussed the importance of reading beyond literal understanding and of examining the author's message from another perspective.

Over the next few days, I used the questions to prompt students' reading of the first three chapters of *Number the Stars*. While reading, students continued to make connections. I was excited to see the connections my students made as they read the chapter. Examples of their connections are featured in Figure 18. They shared their connections with one another and a discussion about rations, soldiers in the streets, and the Danish Resistance followed.

Making these connections was not just important to promoting active comprehension. As the students were able to relate events from the book to their own lives, I could see that they were on their way to viewing the events from a different perspective. Even so, I wanted the students to go further, viewing the author's message from an entirely different perspective.

EXTENDING STUDENTS' THINKING After they had read the first three chapters and had asked questions about whose voice was missing and what alternative stories might have been left out, we engaged in a discussion about imagining the story from different perspectives and how important it is to challenge what we read. We revisited our two Problem Posing questions, and the students worked with a partner to discuss and record their responses.

FIGURE 18

EXAMPLES OF STUDENTS' PERSONAL CONNECTIONS TO *NUMBER THE STARS*

Story Event	Student Connections
Kirsti wanted to hear a story.	I love to hear stories.
Annemarie was telling Kirsti fairy tales	My brother used to read me fairy tales.
Kirsti liked cupcakes.	I like cupcakes.
She remembered her father talking about other countries.	I talk about Iraq with my dad.
Annemarie used to sit on her father's lap when she was little.	I sat in my father's lap when I was little.
Annemarie's sister died.	My grandmother died. I have family members who died.
Annemarie has a Jewish friend.	I have Jewish friends.
Ellen and Annemarie walk together.	Kate and I walk together.
This story happened during World War II.	We are living during the Iraq War.

Next, we discussed whose viewpoints were missing and how the story would change if those viewpoints had been included. The students suggested different ideas. Several, including Marta, James, Tommy, and Ben, thought that the soldier's voice was missing and that including it would have changed the tone of the story. Others, including Pam, Jaffe, Jerry, and Louisa, focused on the mothers and noted how the story would have changed if either of them had told the story of Jews being taken away by the Germans. Finally, Everene and Diane suggested that several voices were missing. These included the soldier, the mothers, Peter, Kirsti, and King Christian. Sam noted that all of those perspectives could be represented in the novel if each chapter were told from a different perspective. Students responded positively to this idea and said that way we could see how each of those people viewed the story.

To further extend their thinking about the first three chapters of *Number the Stars,* students created Mind and Alternative Mind Portraits (McLaughlin & Allen, 2002b) representing two different characters' perspectives. Figure 19 presents portraits of Kirsti and the soldier, completed by Alison and Jason. When the portraits were finished, the students in small groups shared the perspectives of the people who were left out of the book, and we displayed the portraits in our classroom.

REFLECTION *Number the Stars* is a part of our curriculum, and the students truly enjoy reading it. It was a particularly interesting experience this year because we read it from a

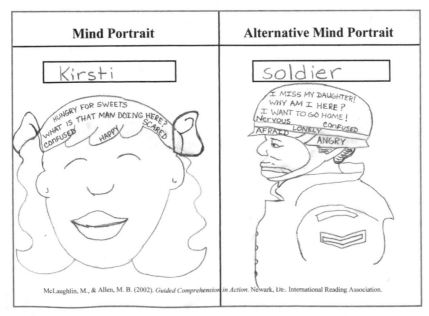

McLaughlin, M., & Allen, M. B. (2002). *Guided Comprehension in Action.* Newark, DE. International Reading Association.

FIGURE 19

critical stance. When we finished reading the novel and discussing its critical perspectives, we decided to invite an author, who is also a Holocaust survivor, to visit our classroom and share his experiences.

FINAL NOTES ON THE *NUMBER THE STARS* LESSON There are three important goals Amy achieves in her lesson to shift student thinking from the book to seeing beyond the text. First, she gives the students permission to see beyond the text by making student input about the topic the first item on the lesson agenda and, therefore, powerful. Second, she shifts discussion from the book itself to using the book to discuss the topic of World War II and the Holocaust. Third, after empowering students' input and establishing the primacy of the topic over the book, she is able to discuss different viewpoints about World War II and the Holocaust. A closer look at these three points follows.

First, we must consider that in most classrooms, teachers stress the importance of literal understandings of the text by repeatedly asking questions about details in the text and requesting that students write retellings of the book. In these contexts, discussions straying very far from the text would be considered off-topic and inappropriate. When this happens, students begin to focus increasingly on ideas in the book and find it more difficult to see beyond or behind the text. In critical literacy, it is important that students be knowledgeable about the text but not feel they have to limit discussions to the ideas as they are represented in the text. In order to see things from a different perspective, students must feel that they have permission to think beyond the text.

With the goal of getting students to see beyond the text, Amy does a beautiful job of first distinguishing between "book knowledge" of the Holocaust in *Number the Stars* and the students' own background knowledge, having separate discussions about each body of knowledge. She shakes the students' dependency on the ideas in the text and highlights the importance of the students' own knowledge by starting with the facts students know about World War II and the Holocaust. She further draws attention to student knowledge by asking them to make connections. In this way, student knowledge outside the book gains status compared with information inside the book. This gives students permission to explore using their own knowledge about the text. It transfers some of the power over to the students, putting their ideas on equal footing and allowing them to think about the story from different perspectives.

By discussing the topics of World War II and the Holocaust and bringing in a Holocaust survivor, Amy shifts the focus of the discussion from discussing information about the book to discussing information about the topic. Once it became clear that discussion was not limited by the ideas in the text, students "could" then use the information from the book as a tool to think about perspectives on World War II and the Holocaust. However, just because students "could" think about this information in a different way, didn't mean that they "would" look at it in a different way. The ground had been fertilized and the critical literacy seed questions guided students to see beyond the text.

After posing questions about whose voice is missing or discounted and about alternative viewpoints, Amy's class begins to see beyond the text. The Mind and Alternative Mind Portraits extend and reinforce students understanding that the topics of World War II and the Holocaust can be told from different perspectives.

Amy's class's comprehension of *Number the Stars* involves more than understanding the story or its characters. By looking at alternative perspectives, their comprehension of the story takes on multi-layered and complex meanings, allowing the students to extend beyond the author's reach. Perhaps more importantly, they learn that stories they hear and tell others usually represent a single perspective that is only part of the story. When they are really honest with themselves and others, they know that the truth comes in different colors, shapes, and sizes, and from different sides of the fence. So, as the students read other texts with a single view, they will know how to understand the event from a range of perspectives. The students will no longer be naïve or simplistic in their understanding of events. After they have gained the skill of challenging the text with questions and understanding at a much more complex level, they may come to understand their own actions and biases as well as others' perspectives on life.

CRITICAL LITERACY LESSON

BOOK: *The Wretched Stone*
TEACHER: Tom Flowers
GRADE: 6

TEXT SYNOPSIS In this picture book by Chris Van Allsburg, a captain and his creative sailors set out on a journey long ago. At first they are dancing, playing instruments, and reciting poetry, but after encountering an odd rock on an island, they lose all their creative abilities and just watch the glowing stone. Eventually, after locking themselves into the forward hold of the ship to watch the wretched stone (which is often interpreted to be a television), they turn into apes. They turn back into people only after the captain reads to them and plays music.

GETTING STARTED Tom read a picture book to his class and afterward asked them to consider several questions listed on chart paper as a way to disrupt the commonplace, see things from a different perspective, and take action. He did this several times with different books to try to establish those questions as common ways students could challenge the ideas of the text. When he thought his students were comfortable using the questions to challenge the text, he chose *The Wretched Stone* as the text on which to base the following lesson.

ENGAGING STUDENTS' THINKING Prior to our reading of *The Wretched Stone*, we had read *The Giving Tree* and *The Battle of Gettysburg* and examined from a critical perspective advertisements from the newspaper. Students had already questioned: *Who was in the text and who was missing? What was the author trying to make me think? What might be an alternative text? What action will I take now that I understand this picture/story in a different way?* I reviewed these ideas with my students and introduced *The Wretched Stone*, which I had chosen because the book takes such a strong and controversial stand on issues that affect all of our students' lives—television and computer games. We briefly discussed the cover and title, and they made some predictions.

GUIDING STUDENTS' THINKING I wanted all of my students to enjoy the story, so I read the book to them and then we discussed it in a general way. Next, we orally retold the story so that I could make sure the students understood it. Then I reminded the students that beyond the literal meaning of Van Allsburg's text, there were meanings at a symbolic level. I reread the description of the wretched stone—"…two feet across, a portion of it is as flat and smooth as glass. From this surface comes a glowing light that is quite beautiful and pleasing to look at (p. 10)"—and I asked the students to consider what they thought the wretched stone represented in our day. Before responding to that thought, I prompted them to remember that the sailors on the ship were lively and fun when they read, danced, played instruments, and told stories, but when the sailors watched the stone, they turned into apes.

To guide the students' critical understanding of the text, we revisited a chart that contained several questions we had been using to critically analyze texts:

◆ Who or what is the focus in the text? Whose viewpoint is expressed?

◆ Whose voices are missing, silenced, or discounted?

- What does the author or text want readers to believe?

- How might alternative perspectives be represented?

- What action might readers take based on what they have learned?

I read each question and then we thought together as a group to see if we could use the questions to create a discussion that might lead to critical understanding of *The Wretched Stone*. For example, the students recognized the wretched stone to be a television, but when I asked them if they were sure it was a television, they said it could also be a computer or Nintendo. Some students thought that the author was correct because sometimes kids get to be very boring when they watch television all the time. But they also said that sometimes the television and computer made them think about jokes or new ways to play with each other. This launched us into a discussion about the correctness of a possible theme of the book and students started talking about an alternative perspective, namely that there are a lot of benefits to television and computers. I could hear emotion in their voice as they complained about Van Allsburg's ideas. Since the students were so engaged in the discussion, I asked them to represent some ideas through improvisational drama, sketching, or written response.

EXTENDING STUDENTS' THINKING To extend their thinking, students wrote their critical views of the text. Most of the students' writings seemed to challenge the author's view that the arts—dancing, storytelling, music—made a person more creative. For example, Bou Thao, an English Language Learner, wrote articulately about the author's purpose and which voices were missing:

> This story is about a group of sailors, who are very creative. They know how to dance and tell stories. The author is trying to make me think watching television is bad and it will make you not smart anymore. People who watch educational channels voices are missing.

The ideas Bou wrote show that not only is he aware of the story's content, but he also has an individual response to the story. His use of the concept of "voices" illustrates that he is comfortable using some of the vocabulary of critical literacy.

In the following example, Ricky, another student, used some complex language. He also seems passionate about challenging the author:

> ## This Book Implies the Fact That Books Are Good and TV Is Bad!
>
> The book titled *The Wretched Stone* is trying to imply that all books make you active and TV will turn you into a non-thinking animal. What about *Sesame Street?* And how about books on how to make bombs and stuff? Not all books are good and not all TV is bad. The author refuses to realize the truth about life. TV and entertainment isn't bad, it's how you use it.

Using his own examples, Ricky has been able to restate the author's theme or purpose and argue against books in favor of some of the good qualities of television. Finally, he comes to a conclusion that was not mentioned in the discussion—that the media are not bad; it's how we use the media.

REFLECTION When teaching students about developing a critical perspective, it seemed that the analysis that produced critical understanding of the text required that the students first have a literal and then a symbolic understanding of the text. After the students understood those two layers of the text, they could begin to challenge the truthfulness of the author's statement. For my students, critical understanding was yet another layer of thinking beyond the literal and symbolic meaning of the text. It was exciting to try to understand the purposes and meanings behind the writing of the text. It was as if the students were detectives or psychologists trying to figure out what the author was thinking and then evaluating that.

FINAL NOTES ON THE *WRETCHED STONE* LESSON In contrast to students who simply summarize the reading, the students in Tom Flowers's class had a discussion with the ideas of the author. As critical readers, they no longer merely replicated information but disrupted the typical classroom process of restating the official knowledge and gave voice to multiple perspectives.

How Challenging the Text Becomes Critical Understanding

It is obvious to most people who have taught in the classroom that in order for teachers to anchor these critical thoughts in the heads of students, the teacher must explain and model the questions and then engage the students in using them on multiple occasions. Readers acquire the habit of challenging the text with questions only after doing so many times over the course of years. The above lessons are good starting points from which we can all begin to learn how to challenge the text.

Problem Posing, when used to disrupt the commonplace or challenge accepted themes, is an effective way to help students go beyond literal comprehension to a deeper level of critical understanding. In Denise White's class, students had heard the story *No, David!* many times, always apparently enjoying the pictures and the text at a literal knowledge level. When Denise asked the students to think about who was doing the talking in the story and who was not, the students began to elaborate the mother's voice, telling us about her intentions and justified fears. This was a different viewpoint from the sharp, negative mother who appears to be frantic and tense. Later, one student revised the mother's image by drawing her as a much more agreeable person than she appears to be in the book. Students also elaborated on the pictures in the text and began to imagine David's viewpoint as "he thinks he won't break anything." In this case, Problem Posing served to help students question David's and his mother's thoughts beyond the text and that helped them elaborate and revise the characters.

Cathleen Perez asked students not only to understand what the author was trying to convey (theme) but also to question the author's message of sharing and create an alternative view of the text—*Should we try to buy our friends?* Such questions began to challenge the author as the authority in the book and gave students permission to think in different ways, disrupting the commonplace and suggesting that even though the author had implied an interpretation, the readers were also free to construct their differences with the author and reinterpret the story. Voicing a difference of opinion from the author or any adult is a developmental leap for most second graders, who are usually very dependent on adults. From a critical literacy perspective, it shows a confidence about the importance of understanding different ideas and valuing freedom of thought.

Amy Homeyer's fifth grade sought to disrupt the common understandings of *Number the Stars* by envisioning the story from the mothers' and the soldiers' points of view. The story already carefully detailed by the author became contested ground as students began to imagine different events, different perspectives, and different tones for the story.

Finally, after students understood *The Wretched Stone* on the symbolic level and began to pose questions challenging the author's message that television makes people less thoughtful, they began to problematize (see Appendix A) book reading and television watching. Ricky points out that the issue is not that simple. Television can be educational (*Sesame Street*) and books ("about bombs") can lead to tragedy. There is excitement and passion when Ricky responds. He expresses his view with exclamation points and by raising challenging questions for the author.

Final Thoughts on This Theme

In these lessons, readers not only came to understand the literal and symbolic messages that the author communicated but also came to engage the authors in some intellectual jousting, challenging their ideas and mounting support for their own. Through Problem Posing, the students became readers who were open to other perspectives and possible new events and tones.

The story no longer belonged only to the author but rather became a fluid, shifting event that changed depending on the readers' desire to assert his or her own background knowledge and engage in a reconstruction of the story.

In the next chapter, the students' critical understanding continues to grow as they speculate about the multifaceted nature of identity. We investigate identities and again have the opportunity to "sit in on" a variety of critical literacy lessons at the primary, intermediate, and middle school levels.

Critical Literacy: Enhancing Students' Comprehension of Text

CHAPTER 4

Exploring Identities

"One of the things I've noticed is that my students have learned a lot about the power they have as readers. They are more actively engaged in their reading, and, at this point, seem to naturally question what the author wants us to believe. It has taken time, but they have moved beyond saying, 'It's a good book' and have discovered new ways of understanding."

LESLIE FISHER, first grade teacher

When Leslie shared her thoughts about her students, everyone in the group agreed that their students also seemed to have a stronger sense of themselves and a stronger sense of their power as readers. This led us into an interesting discussion of the theme of identity and how our critical literacy experiences had impacted our individual identities.

We acknowledged that identity is personal. It defines who we are and who we are not. We also talked about identity as a social process and observed that much of who we are and who we are not is constructed through our reading, our everyday experiences, and the conversations we have with others. For example, a girl who reads about Little Red Riding Hood might identify with that character and believe that her dominant roles are to be cute, to avoid trouble by staying on the path and doing the right thing, to take care of grandmother and others, and to call for help if she is in trouble. A girl reading a teen magazine may be influenced by what teen girls are supposed to be concerned about: beauty, fame, and romance. The masculine identity provides another clear example. For some, the masculine identity is constructed in truck commercials or football games as a person who is serious, powerful, and tough. For others, the masculine identity is constructed in texts that portray men as being kind, thoughtful, or funny.

These examples illustrate that there is a wide range of identities, but the reality is that each person has a range of identities beyond gender, such as teacher, parent, friend, or athlete, that are formed through interaction with texts and our social world (our relationships with others). We often merely accept—without question—roles we see constructed in texts and in other events. But people who are critically aware challenge the socially constructed roles so that neither they nor others are unjustly limited.

When exploring identities, readers who are critically aware read beyond the text and examine influences that shape our sense of self—who we are, what we do, how we speak. These influences on our identity are mostly hidden and not evident to the casual reader. Our task as readers is to be critical about the roles of the characters in the text and to uncover the stereotyping of roles for gender, race, age, ethnic group, religion, national identity, and other categories so that we will not passively accept those stereotypes for ourselves or others.

In this chapter our exploration of identities enters the classroom as teachers share critical literacy lessons that focus on exploring identities at the primary, intermediate, and middle school levels. To draw the chapter to a close, we reflect on the outcomes of examining identities from a critical perspective.

Classroom Lessons in Which Readers Explore Identities

This section features a variety of lessons in which students analyze and challenge socially constructed identities in texts at the primary, intermediate, and middle school levels. They disrupt common roles by changing what the main characters do or by imagining them in a different way. They discuss the new identities and how they would impact the story. And, finally, they transfer the new identities to other situations in life and take action based on what they have learned.

As discussed in Chapter 2, the teachers who designed and taught these lessons used a planning format that focused on engaging, guiding, and extending students' thinking. Each of the lessons is described in the teacher's own words. The narratives include text descriptions and feature examples of student work. Figure 20 provides an overview of the lessons, including the instructional level, text, and strategy focus.

FIGURE 20

OVERVIEW OF LESSONS IN THE EXPLORING IDENTITIES THEME

LEVEL	TEXT	EXPLORING IDENTITIES CRITICAL FOCUS
Primary	*The Fourth Little Pig*	Critical Conversations Gender Issues
Primary	*Jack and the Beanstalk*	Critical Questions Heroes and Villains
Intermediate	*When Jessie Came Across the Sea*	Multiple Perspectives Family, Age, Immigration
Middle School	*A Picnic in October* *Bearstone*	Multiple Perspectives Family, Age, Immigration Juxtapositioning narrative Numerous informational articles and informational text from websites Alternative Perspectives

BOOK: *The Fourth Little Pig*
TEACHER: Karolyn Martin
GRADE: 1

TEXT SYNOPSIS In this version of the classic fairy tale, the sister, Pig Four, arrives at the brick house to find her three brothers locked inside, safe from the threat of the big, bad wolf. She tells them that they cannot spend their whole lives hiding in the house and that they need to get out and experience life. The brothers continue to refuse to go outside. Frustrated by their stubbornness, Pig Four huffs and puffs and blows their house down. When the brothers find themselves outdoors and realize the wolf is not there, they go off to enjoy life. The sister, Pig Four, takes a different path and goes off to explore the world.

GETTING STARTED After reading an alternative version of a popular fairy tale and comparing the original and alternative version of *The Three Little Pigs* using a Venn diagram, Karolyn read yet another version of the story with a Gender Switch (see Chapter 2) in which a fourth pig was a girl. The analysis of the juxtaposition of those three stories and the Gender Switch yielded discussions about the sex-role stereotyping of boys and girls.

ENGAGING STUDENTS' THINKING I knew my students were already familiar with alternative perspectives because we had read transformational fairy tales, such as *The True Story of the 3 Little Pigs!,* as part of our unit of study. I began by engaging the students in a retelling of the original version of *The Three Little Pigs.* Next, we focused on the characters in the story to see if they had any stereotypical traits and to see if we could come up with some alternative characters or traits for the characters. We revisited the Venn diagram to compare and contrast the original story and *The True Story of the 3 Little Pigs!* We discussed the information we had recorded about the pigs and the wolf in each story. Next, we discussed the number of pigs there had been in the stories we had already read and talked about how the pigs had been represented. Student responses centered on the fact that there were three pigs in both stories and that they were brothers. They were all "boy pigs." Then I introduced *The Fourth Little Pig.*

GUIDING STUDENTS' THINKING As soon as the students heard the title and saw the cover, they appeared very surprised that there was a "girl pig" on the cover. They were very eager to hear what role she would play in the story.

As I read the story aloud, I encouraged students to think about how this story was similar to and different from the other versions we had read. Because the story has a rhyming format and a limited amount of text, it was a quick read. After my first reading, we had a brief discussion about what happened in the story. After my second reading, students worked with a partner to discuss the similarities and differences. Then we shared ideas in a whole-class setting. Students' ideas about things that were similar to the other stories included that there were pigs in all of the stories, there were brick houses in some of the stories, and all of the stories had happy endings. They also determined some interesting differences between *The Fourth Little Pig* and the other books. These included that the story seemed to occur after the other stories and that the three little pigs were hiding in the brick house, still afraid of the wolf. Most of the students thought the greatest difference was that this book featured the sister—a "girl pig." I used that observation as a springboard for examining the notion of identity and how it helps us read from a critical stance.

EXTENDING STUDENTS' THINKING We began by discussing the role the sister, Pig Four, played in *The Fourth Little Pig*. The following is an excerpt from our conversation:

Teacher:	You have told me that the sister, Pig Four, being in this story was what was different from the other stories about the three little pigs. What are some things that Pig Four, the sister, did in this story?
Nora:	She was trying to help her brothers.
Salvatore:	She wanted them to go outside and not be afraid of the wolf now.
Teacher:	What are some things the sister did to get her brothers to leave their locked brick house and go outside?
Beth:	She told them. She said they should.
Cody:	But that didn't make them go.
Matt:	They didn't really go. She huffed and puffed and blew the house down. When the house fell down, they were outside.
Dawn:	Yes, she huffed and puffed and the house fell down.

Cristin:	But in the other stories it was the wolf that huffed and puffed.
Michael:	Yeah, girl pigs can't huff and puff and make houses fall down.
Susan:	Well, girl pigs might not really be able to, but she did it in the story.
Teacher:	What are some things you think girls can do?

Students' responses were wide-ranging. They began with go to school, go out to play, watch television, and dance, and moved on to read, use computers, and play sports. When I asked what sports girls can play, the students responded somewhat traditionally

FIGURES 21 & 22

at first. Then Dawn said, "Girls can play football. I play football with my family in our yard." Dawn's statement led us to a much broader base of responses about sports and many other aspects of life and, eventually, to Nick's observation that "girls can do everything!"

We extended our thinking by making a class mural that depicted girls and boys playing sports, working on projects, and engaging in a variety of professions (medicine, construction, business). We adapted Nick's observation and placed it at the center of our mural: Girls and boys can do everything! Examples of students' contributions to our mural can be seen in Figures 21 and 22.

REFLECTION I was proud to see my students reason through this gender issue. As is often the case, discussion at this level can be time consuming, but the outcome was well worth the investment. In a subsequent lesson, students made thoughtful connections to "girl characters" in other stories, including *Cinderella* and *Goldilocks and the Three Bears*. The students clearly viewed the sister, Pig Four, as empowered. As Cathy, one of my students, observed, "Cinderella and Goldilocks needed help. Pig Four was a helper."

FINAL NOTES ON THE *FOURTH LITTLE PIG* LESSON In these lessons critical literacy focused on issues of reflection, transformation, and action, using alternative viewpoints of a traditional folktale. With the introduction of a fourth little pig, the students listening to the story begin to challenge or disrupt ideas, not merely as an exercise to understand a fairy tale, but rather as an event in which the identity of girls is socially constructed by the group. What are girls like? What should they be able to do and what are they unable to do? The challenge for all in the group is to think about the limits of gender and to challenge hidden assumptions students have about them. Because the challenge occurs in a discussion about a story, students may feel freer to discuss the ways they limit themselves and others into gender-stereotyped roles.

As a result of that discussion and the mural extension, boys and girls may have a new understanding of what it means to be a boy or girl, but we can only assume action will be taken as a result of the students' new understanding. The teacher has given the students the intellectual tools of critical analysis, including analysis, naming the sex-role stereotype, and reflection. The analysis and naming of the sex-role stereotypes in the first two books raises the issue of the identity, ability, and power of girls. This class reflection will help students identify situations in their own lives in which girls might be limited, and the discussion will give students the words to articulate the injustice.

BOOK: *Jack and the Beanstalk*

TEACHER: Kimber Pauls

GRADE: 2

TEXT SYNOPSIS Kimber Pauls read *Jack and the Beanstalk* to engage her students in critical literacy. In this classic fairy tale, poor Jack sells his cow for some magic beans that grow a beanstalk to the clouds where the giant and his wife live. Jack steals from the threatening giant the hen that lays the golden eggs, as well as some money. In the end, Jack escapes down the beanstalk and cuts down the beanstalk with the giant on it, and the giant is killed.

GETTING STARTED Kimber chose a story in which the main character, who is assumed to be a hero, does some unheroic deeds. After contrasting the actions (identities) of hero and villain, Kimber posed the question, "Who was the hero?" She persisted in asking that question as she reread the story, pausing occasionally where appropriate and urging the students to compare the fairy tale character with the students' descriptions of hero and villain.

ENGAGING STUDENTS' THINKING I wanted to start my second grade students off with a familiar story for their first experience with critical literacy, so I selected the story of *Jack and the Beanstalk*. Before I read the story to the class, I asked them what they remembered about it. Next, I wrote on the board "Heroes" and "Villains" and asked the students who they thought the hero was in *Jack and the Beanstalk*. They immediately agreed that Jack was the hero or "good guy" in the story and, consequently, the giant was the villain or, as they preferred to call him, "the bad guy." I asked them to share descriptions of what they thought a hero was. They said a hero is the kind of person who "rescues somebody" or "saves someone." Then I asked the students to share descriptions of what they thought a villain was. Students gave me answers such as "a bad person" and "someone who does bad things." It was at this point in the discussion that I asked, "Which is Jack in the story—a hero or a villain?" "Which is the giant?" "Which is the giant's wife?" I reminded the students that Jack stole three things from the giant: the gold, the hen, and the harp.

Then they reflected on whether they considered Jack's actions to be right or wrong. Again, I asked the class if they thought that Jack was a hero or a villain. This time the class was much more hesitant in responding. One student pointed out that the giant was bad because he wanted to eat Jack. At this point in the lesson, the majority of the class was in agreement that the giant was a villain, but there was a definite uncertainty about whether Jack was a hero or another villain.

GUIDING STUDENTS' THINKING I read the story of *Jack and the Beanstalk* aloud to the class. When I came to the part of the story where Jack steals the bag of gold, I paused and gave the students a moment to let that part of the story sink in. Then I asked them, "Who owns the gold?" Many of the students answered that the gold belongs to the giant. I asked the class if it was right for Jack to steal the gold. Those who answered agreed that it wasn't right for Jack to steal the gold because it belonged to the giant. Throughout the reading of the story I would pause and question my students to get their feedback on what they thought of Jack's actions. As the story progressed, it was clear the students were beginning to see that Jack was not really a "good guy" type of a hero because he took not only the giant's material possessions, but his life as well.

EXTENDING STUDENTS' THINKING At the end of the story, we discussed the roles of the other characters in *Jack and the Beanstalk*. The students still viewed the giant as a villain because he threatened to eat Jack and he was intent on pursuing Jack to kill him at the climax of the story. Jack's mother was considered by most of my students as a neutral character, but some kids thought that she was mean because she called Jack an "idiot" and "stupid" when she discovered that Jack sold the cow for five beans. The students considered the giant's wife to be one of the "good" people in the story because she tried to warn Jack about her dangerous husband, and she provided food for Jack when he was hungry.

For the next step, the students reflected and wrote about what they thought of the story of *Jack and the Beanstalk* and elaborated on what they thought of Jack's actions in the story. I encouraged them to draw and write about their ideas. When I collected the students' responses, I found that eleven students pointed out that Jack had stolen from the giant and five of those students had described Jack as "not nice" or "bad." Four students wrote that the giant's wife was "nice" and that she was a "hero." Examples of drawings and descriptions by students who thought that "Jack was not nice," "Jack is a bad guy," and "Jack stole the harp" are featured in Figures 23, 24, and 25.

Jack was not nice because He steals the gold and He steals the golden hen.

Jack is a bad guy. He steals the hen and harp and gold. He kills the giant. They lived together.

by Itself

Jack was a bad Prsen. Jack Steals The harp Jack went down The binstok and Jack Told his mom two Brey The axe and Jack Jop down The binstok and They levd happlex

FIGURES 23, 24, 25

REFLECTION I was pleased with how the class got involved with the opening discussion about the heroes and villains. I also felt that the critical discussions we had during the reading of *Jack and the Beanstalk* went well. All of the students who said Jack was a hero shifted their understanding of Jack to be a "bad" person who "steals the gold and the harp" "and the hen" and "kills the giant." After we identified the attributes of a hero and a villain, none of the children called Jack a hero, as they had before.

FINAL NOTES ON THE *JACK AND THE BEANSTALK* LESSON The students' traditional identification with the main character of a story as the "good" guy is challenged in Kimber Pauls's classroom as students analyze the story and discover Jack behaves in ways the children find to be "bad." In recognizing that Jack is foregrounded in the text, and receives most of the author's attention, students come to understand that the main character might in fact do "bad" things. This disrupts their understanding of story grammar and provides them with a different point of view concerning how goodness is constructed. In this story, students refuse to characterize Jack as a hero because of his "bad" behavior. Consequently, the concept of goodness that is being socially constructed in this story, and in the classroom, is altered by the students' critical understanding of Jack.

Although it is not clear how much these lessons spilled over into children's thinking and actions in their daily lives, it does become clear that the children are using this text to challenge and make decisions about what makes up the identity of a hero. Perhaps students drew on the discussion of "hero" as they viewed their Superman comics or experienced the actions of a friend on the playground. Perhaps Kimber used the discussion later on to analyze a real-life event on the playground. In any case, the intellectual tools of analysis of identity (heroes and villains) gives students the skills, the encouragement, and the permission to disrupt the author's intentions. The naming of Jack as "bad" and the process of analysis give students the skills and the words to take action in the future.

CRITICAL LITERACY LESSON

BOOK: *When Jessie Came Across the Sea*
TEACHER: Mary Roehrenbeck
GRADE: 5

TEXT SYNOPSIS Written by Amy Hest, this is the story of a young girl who was chosen to use a free ticket to America to escape the plight of the poor village in which she lived. Unable to bear the thought of leaving her grandmother, Jessie leaves her prized possession with her grandmother in the hope that they will one day be reunited. The book is written from Jessie's perspective.

GETTING STARTED Mary read a few books about immigration, visited several websites, and heard information about particular immigrants and about students' visits to Ellis Island as background to subsequent discussions. (For information about the websites, see "Immigration" in Appendix C.) Focusing on one book, Mary and her students discussed immigration from the perspectives of different people affected by it. Simulated letters home were written by "immigrants," and a play displaying multiple perspectives was written and performed—all as a way to help students understand different viewpoints on immigration.

ENGAGING STUDENTS' THINKING I motivated students by reading *Coming to America* to provide a multicultural view of America as a "nation of immigrants." Then I engaged them in a discussion of immigrants in general and Annie Moore, the first immigrant to set foot on Ellis Island. Next, to build background knowledge about how immigrants feel when moving to a new country, students wrote about times when they felt like outsiders, or when people made judgments about them based on things over which they had no control (see Figure 26). We shared these in small groups and then discussed them with the whole class.

Then we had a class discussion, connecting immigration in the past to the feelings of immigrants in America today. We talked about what it must have been like to journey all the way to America long ago only to be turned back because of illness. We also discussed in what ways we would have tried to make the immigrants of the past, who may have felt like outsiders, feel welcome. Finally, we thought about what we could do to make today's immigrants feel welcome.

FIGURE 26

FEELING LIKE AN OUTSIDER

On the first day of school last year, I felt like an outsider. I was new at this school and I felt like I didn't fit in at all. I remember being shy and nervous and I didn't talk a lot that day. It was so different from what I knew. Everyone except me seemed to belong here. Everyone seemed to know everyone else and what they should do. I could tell that this was going to be different from my old school and I was scared. On that day I thought I would never fit in. Whenever I think about what it means to be an outsider, I always think of that day.

GUIDING STUDENTS' THINKING I introduced *When Jessie Came Across the Sea* as a story of immigration. I shared the title and cover and we briefly discussed the book. I noted that the book was written from Jessie's perspective and encouraged students to think about that perspective as well as the perspectives of the other characters as they listened to me read the book aloud. Then I read to the students, stopping periodically to discuss the story with them.

EXTENDING STUDENTS' THINKING When I finished reading, we began discussing the different perspectives from which the story could have been written. To ensure that students understood this dimension of critical literacy, they worked with partners and wrote letters from the point of view of Jessie's grandmother before she knew she would be able to join Jessie in America (see Figure 27). This perspective represented the feelings of those left behind by family members. From this perspective, students were able to make connections to the plights of both groups of people—the immigrants and those who could not or would not leave their native country. This activity encouraged students to reason through and come to understand the feelings of immigrants and their determination to make their new lives work.

Students further extended their thinking by working in groups to develop a script and dramatize what they learned about immigration and Ellis Island. They represented multiple perspectives of the immigration process, including family members left behind, the immigrant(s) at various stages of their journey, the immigrant(s) at various ages, the captain of the ship, the people meeting the immigrant(s) in America, those who tried to immigrate but were denied access because they failed inspection, the medical inspector, and employers in America. The students and I enthusiastically agreed that the dramatizations were impressive. Figure 28 delineates the perspective of a potential immigrant who was denied access. Figure 29 shows a moment in the dramatization when students, representing immigrants who were denied access, held signs depicting the chalk letters that were written on clothing to indicate the potential immigrant had an illness.

REFLECTION Student response to these lessons was powerful. This topic was of high interest to both my students and their parents. It was obvious that learning about immigration and Ellis Island continued after school because of the unassigned research that my students did at home. Excursions to Ellis Island were also taken by several students and information from the journeys was enthusiastically shared with class members. Students seemed especially to appreciate depicting the various phases of the immigration process

LETTERS FROM JESSIE'S GRANDMOTHER

Dear Jessie,

I have really been missing you! How was your trip to the new world? I am so happy you arrived safely. Are the streets of America really paved with gold? I have been spending some time practicing the writing you taught me. I think I am getting good at it. What do you think? Did you make any new laces or dresses lately? Miss Minney is still skinny like always, but she is doing well. I hope you like your new life. I miss you too and wish we could be together again. Always remember that you don't have to see me to love me. Keep me in your heart and I will keep you in mine.

Love,
Grandma

Dear Jessie,

It was so good to hear from you. I miss you too, but I am happy to know things are good for you. The young man you wrote about seems like a good person. I can tell that you like him. Everyone here misses you. We all want to sail across the ocean and be with you. I sometimes worry that we won't see each other again before I pass away. I hope we will. Until then, we can be close in our letters.

Love,
Grandma

Dear Jessie,

I was so excited when I opened your letter! I am so happy that you are going to be married! And I am even happier that you sent me a ticket so I can come to America for the wedding. I have already started packing and getting ready for the boat. Saying goodbye to my friends is hard, but I keep thinking that I will be seeing you again soon. I cannot wait! Seeing you again will be my greatest joy.

Love,
Grandma

102 Critical Literacy: Enhancing Students' Comprehension of Text

FIGURE 28

IMMIGRANT DENIED ACCESS

We are on Ellis Island and slowly make our way into the great hall. I am nervous. Sweat trickles down my forehead. It is my turn. I sit down in a chair. A man checks me for trachoma. The button hook flips my eyelid. I yell in agony, but then the examination is over. Just as I am about to walk through to where my family is waiting, the man grabs his chalk and writes "E" on my jacket. Other immigrants look at me horrified. My family slumps their heads in sorrow as I am taken down to the storage area. I see immigrants moaning and having hysterical fits of crying. I am dragged to my cell.

The next morning I feel terrible. "Wake up, people!" the guards shout. As we leave Ellis Island, a piece of my jacket gets caught in the door and I turn and take my last glimpse of the Statue of Liberty. I sob knowing I have nothing to go back to. I remember the first time I saw the Statue of Liberty. I saw hope and freedom and a new life. Now I will be returned to Russia and never know hope and freedom. I remember the crowded ship we took to America. I remember how it felt to stand on American soil. I remember my last look at my family and my night in the storage cell. Then I say goodbye to the land of hope and opportunity.

FIGURE 29

FIGURE 30

and taking on the perspectives of those involved. "Immigration officials" recognized the importance of not spreading disease in America and clashed with the immigrants' desires and their concept of America as a welcoming land. The dialogue that ensued was amazing. The students were able to articulate key information about the immigration process and work within the perspectives they represented. It was gratifying to see that they not only understood the different points of view, but also took ownership of them. Figures 30 and 31 contain photographs taken during the dramatizations.

By the time the unit was over, I knew my students were comfortable reading from a critical perspective. They were analyzing the perspectives of all involved in the process, probing authors' messages, and questioning the power relationships involved in the immigration process.

FINAL NOTES ON THE *WHEN JESSIE CAME ACROSS THE SEA* LESSON Not satisfied with a simplistic explanation of immigration, Mary Roehrenbeck challenged students to recognize the complexity of all the identities of different people involved in immigration. Perhaps for some of the students, the knowledge that people were rejected from immigration because of sickness complicates and disrupts their understanding of America as a land of immigrants. This investigation into the multiple meanings of immigration and the increased complexity of the knowledge students have about immigration is an excellent example of how to problematize an event so that students understand it from more perspectives and in more detail than they understood previously (see Appendix A). Students were also able to articulate power relationships between the identities of the characters: immigrants and officials.

It is important to note that there are many instances in our society in which it is entirely appropriate for people to play a power role over others—for example, as teachers, as coaches, as police, as parents. Any leader of a group of people has to have some kind of authority. Nevertheless, the right to wield power and the extent to which an authority should wield power must be questioned and negotiated lest the power be abusive and lead to injustice and unfairness. The goal of critical literacy is to question the power relations to see if their exercise is legitimate and fair. As teachers and students challenge each other to arrive at a more sophisticated understanding of the legitimate and illegitimate uses of power, they are problematizing the concept of power and authority.

Finally, recognizing the lack of power of immigrants, students discussed action steps toward social justice when they talked about how to welcome immigrants and make their entry a bit easier.

FIGURE 31

BOOK: *A Picnic in October*

TEACHER: Stephanie Romano

GRADE: 5

TEXT SYNOPSIS In this book by Eve Bunting, Tony, the main character, goes with his family on an annual outing to the Statue of Liberty to celebrate his grandmother's birthday. Over time, Tony comes to realize his identity is rooted in his Italian-American heritage. He understands the importance of Lady Liberty not only to his family but also to other immigrants.

GETTING STARTED After encouraging students to briefly share family immigration experiences, the class Stephanie was teaching read a story. Then students made personal connections to the book, interviewed members of their families, and wrote oral histories for the purpose of sharing different, more positive views of the character of the immigrant.

ENGAGING STUDENTS' THINKING To engage students, I invited them to discuss with a partner where their ancestors originally came from. After the students discussed this for a few minutes, we shared in a whole-class setting and noted the various countries on the classroom map of the world. Then we listened to the song "Coming to America" by Neil Diamond. After listening to the lyrics, we began to predict what it might have been like for our ancestors when they journeyed from their homelands to America.

GUIDING STUDENTS' THINKING I introduced the book and we engaged in a brief discussion about the title and cover. Before beginning to read *A Picnic in October*, I encouraged students to make personal connections with the text as they listened to me read. Prompts that I provided included the following:

◆ How do you celebrate your parents', grandparents', or guardians' birthdays?

◆ What traditions or celebrations do you and your family have? What are those times like?

◆ Do you go on picnics or other outings? When? Who participates? What do you think about them?

- Have you ever visited the Statue of Liberty? Would you like to visit it and have a picnic there? Why did Tony's family picnic there?

- Why do you think people continue to leave their homelands to live in countries like America?

While reading, I stopped periodically so the students and I could discuss our personal connections with the text. These included connections to members of family and extended family, family traditions, travels to New York City, and seeing the Statue of Liberty.

EXTENDING STUDENTS' THINKING To help students gain a critical understanding of the text, we focused on multiple perspectives, and the students wrote from an alternative perspective, such as that of Tony's grandmother or another character of their choice. Next, we shared in small groups and discussed in a whole-class setting. An example of the story told from Tony's grandmother's perspective is featured in Figure 32.

I used this activity as a prelude to students' completing long-term Oral History Projects in which the students would explore their identities. They would begin the project by interviewing a grandparent or other member of their family or extended family. We brainstormed questions to guide the interview process and help students gain a deeper sense of their family, its culture, its traditions and, consequently, their own identity. These are some of the questions the students generated to use in their interviews:

- Can you tell me the story of our family's journey to America?

- What are some family traditions that you remember from when you were young?

- What were your favorites?

- Does our family still practice the traditions it did when you were young?

- What are some special places you like to go to? Why do you like to go there?

- What are your favorite foods?

- Is English your first language? Can you speak another language? When did you learn it and how do you use it?

- What do you most enjoy doing with our family? Why?

- If you lived in another land now, would you leave it to come to America?

- How do you feel about being an American?

When the students completed their interviews (see Figure 33), the class hosted a celebration of families in which the students and their relatives participated. During the celebration, the students honored the relatives they had interviewed and shared information about their families and extended families.

FIGURE 32

PICNIC IN OCTOBER FROM THE GRANDMOTHER'S PERSPECTIVE

Every year I celebrate my birthday with my family on Ellis Island. I have done this every year since I came to America. My husband and I meet our family in Battery Park and we all take the ferry out to the Statue of Liberty. Sometimes the ferry lines are long, but I don't care because I remember how long the lines were when I first came to Ellis Island. That was a long time ago and life was very different. I was a little girl and my family and I came from Italy. I was happy to be coming to America, but I was also afraid that everyone in my family might not be let in. We heard stories on the boat about people who were turned away because they were sick or for other reasons. I couldn't believe that could happen. I hoped that wouldn't happen to us. I didn't know what we would do if it did.

I remember feeling relieved when my family and I finally made it through immigration. I remember my father telling us that this was the start of a new life. Every time I see the Statue of Liberty, it reminds me of that day and what my father said. That's why I celebrate my birthday with her. And when I see my grandchildren there with me I know that they will never have to worry about being turned away. They will always have a life of freedom.

FIGURE 33

EXCERPT FROM AN ORAL HISTORY INTERVIEW

1. **What are some traditions your family had when you were young?**

My family came from Poland and when I was younger we would make special foods for the holidays. I remember my grandmother—I was named after her—teaching us how to make *kcrushetci*, and we would help her hang the dough over the backs of chairs to stretch it. Our family would get together and bake special breads in preparation for different holidays. Also, when I was a young girl, we had a tradition of spending Sundays with the whole family at my grandparents' house. That was a long time ago, and life was different. All of the stores were closed on Sundays and a lot of people thought of it as a family day.

2. **Do you still practice those traditions?**

I still do some baking for the holidays, but not as much as my mother and grandmother did. We do still celebrate the holidays with the whole family. And since the malls and other businesses are open on Sunday, it isn't much of a family day anymore. We have maintained holidays as family celebrations and they are still very special.

3. **Do you have a special place you like to go? Where is it? Why is it special for you?**

The beach is my special place. I grew up in the Midwest very far from the ocean, so I never knew the ocean when I was younger. It is special for me because it seems boundless, and watching the rolling waves and walking in the sand seem comforting. I feel free there, like I don't have to worry about a schedule.

4. **Where do you like to celebrate your birthday? Why?**

It doesn't really matter where I celebrate it as long as my family is there to celebrate with me.

5. **How many languages do you speak? How did you learn them?**

I speak three languages. I learned English and Polish as I was growing up. My grandparents spoke only Polish, but they always wanted their descendants to speak English. I learned English from my parents and in school. I learned Spanish in high school.

6. **What do you most enjoy doing with your family? Why?**

I most enjoy cooking all day and then having my family come to dinner. It reminds me of those special family Sundays I had when I was growing up.

7. **How do you feel about being an American? Why?**

I am very proud to be an American. I think we live in the greatest country in the world. I remember when I was a little girl hearing my grandparents talking about what it was like to leave Poland and their families to start a new life here. My grandfather always said, "Our life started with freedom." I always admired them for being so adventurous and making such a courageous move. I wonder if I would have had such courage if I needed to immigrate today.

REFLECTION The students were enthusiastic learners who were actively involved. They wrote from multiple perspectives and extended their understanding of identities to their own lives by participating in the Oral History Project. The celebration of families was a celebration of diversity and acceptance (see Figure 34). Students clearly gained insights into their identities and learned a great deal about others in the process.

FIGURE 34

FINAL NOTES ON *A PICNIC IN OCTOBER* LESSON The typical role of the immigrant in America or elsewhere is often that of lower class and lower status. Americans rush to disassociate themselves from immigrants as soon as possible by calling themselves natives or just plain American. In her reading, discussion, and oral history lesson, Stephanie Romano sought to disrupt that system of thinking by celebrating and raising the status of the immigrant. So the action step in this lesson was to express and celebrate the immigrant in all of us, and in so doing we raise the status and appreciation of immigrants to the benefit of people moving from one place to another. Social justice in this setting means that if you are a recent immigrant, you should not set yourself on a lower level of power relationships with native Americans. Instead you should appreciate your heritage and your family's willingness to move and take on a new home. In addition to the self-conception and status issues, the differences in the immigration experiences led to a more complex understanding of the students' own identities as well as their concept of themselves as Americans.

BOOK: *Bearstone*
TEACHER: Belinda Anderson
GRADE: 8

TEXT SYNOPSIS In this lesson, Belinda used multiple texts: *Bearstone* and several informational articles that she downloaded from the Internet. In *Bearstone*, author Will Hobbs tells the story of Cloyd, a troubled 14-year-old Ute boy, who grows up without parents and is sent by his tribe to live in a group home for Indian boys in the Colorado mountains. When Cloyd is placed in the care of Walter, an old rancher, he discovers the truth about the strength of his heritage, the old man's love, and life.

In addition to *Bearstone*, Belinda used the following informational articles about Andrew Jackson, the Cherokee Trail of Tears, and related topics:

Andrew Jackson's Case for Removal of Indians
<http://www.mtholyoke.edu/intrel/andrew.htm>

The Cherokee Trail of Tears—National Historic Trail—1838–1839
<http://rosecity.net/tears/trail/tearsnht.html>

Stories Along the Trail—The Cherokee Trail of Tears—
Cherokee Indian Slave Story
<http://rosecity.net/tears/trail/slavesty.html>

People of the Colorado Plateau—The Ute Indians
<http://www.cpluhna.nau.edu/People/ute_indians.htm>

Indian Massacre of '74—a Tragedy to Four Sisters
<http://www.rootsweb.com/~nalakota/wotw/indgscstr/germansisters_ tragedy_ baldwin_wotw/indgscstr/indexindgersiscstr.html>

Indian Mascots and Genocide, The Shame of America's Public Schools
<http://www.iwchildren.org/genocide/shame9.htm>

The Mixed Blood Uintas of Utah
<http://www.undeclaredutes.net/Home.htm>

GETTING STARTED Belinda, a somewhat experienced teacher of critical literacy, began engaging students in the topic to be studied and in critical analysis by generating critical questions, using mostly nonfiction texts, many of which originated from the Web. In subsequent days, students studied a range of texts and discussed in small- and whole-group settings the author's intent or purpose for writing. Debates helped clarify the different perspectives and issues at play in the identity of native culture.

ENGAGING STUDENTS' THINKING Before beginning to read *Bearstone*, I wanted to assure myself that my students had background knowledge of related historical topics, so we began by discussing what they already knew about Native Americans, the Cherokee Trail of Tears, and westward expansion during the mid-1800s. Students' responses indicated that although they knew some things about Native Americans, they didn't have much background knowledge of the other two topics. When we discussed Native Americans, Susan said that Native Americans were the original residents of our country and that they were here when the Pilgrims arrived. Gary said he knew that Native Americans used to be called Indians and that they lived in tribes on reservations. Miguel said that he knew that a long time ago, Indians lived where we live now and that a lot of the towns, rivers, and mountains in our area were named after Indian tribes. Joaquin said that his parents had been to a casino that was owned by Native Americans. Other students noted that people they knew had also visited such casinos. Their comments led to a lengthy discussion of who the Native Americans were when the Pilgrims first came to our country, how they were portrayed in movies and television shows about "cowboys and Indians," and how they went from being the original residents of our country to people who live on reservations and own casinos. I used what the students knew about Native Americans to introduce and make connections to the Cherokee Trail of Tears and westward expansion through informational articles I had downloaded from the Internet.

GUIDING STUDENTS' THINKING I distributed the informational articles, giving each group a different title. (Topics addressed included Ute history, Andrew Jackson's proposal to remove the Native Americans from their land, an account of a German family that was massacred while trying to move west, and modern-day perspectives that try to persuade the reader to feel outrage about the treatment of Native Americans today.) Then the students, working in small groups, partner-read and discussed their articles. Students read articles for their content but also to critically analyze the information presented and question what the author intended. I visited each group during this time. Next, we had a whole-class discussion that broadened our knowledge of Native Americans and clarified what we had learned from the articles about the Cherokee Trail of Tears and westward expansion.

Our discussion focused on not only what the articles said but also on who wrote the article, who maintains the website it was downloaded from, why the social studies books included minimal information about these topics, and who decides what is included in text books and what isn't. Our questions were designed to help us understand who created the identity of Native Americans as it was represented in textbooks, in the movies and on television, and in the articles we read. The students noticed right away that the articles provided much more detailed information about the Cherokee Trail of Tears and the impact of westward expansion on Native-American life than their textbooks did, and very different views of Native Americans than the ones generally seen in films or on television.

EXTENDING STUDENTS' THINKING We began extending our thinking by engaging in debates on a number of different topics—Andrew Jackson's beliefs versus Native-American beliefs, society's modern-day perceptions of Native Americans versus Native-Americans' modern-day perceptions of themselves, and determining one's own identity versus having one's identity imposed by society. I wasn't sure how the debate format would work so early in the school year, so I was careful to teach the students about debating and demonstrate how a debate unfolds before asking them to engage in one. The students scaffolded from my model and worked quite well together. The debates were purposeful and enlightening—for my students and myself.

Then we further extended our thinking by writing individual reflections about how the identity of Native Americans is perceived to have changed over time and what has influenced those changes (see Figure 35). We shared these in a whole-class setting and displayed them on the wall outside our classroom, so others could read about the changes Native Americans have experienced.

REFLECTION I wanted to teach the students more about Native Americans—and especially the Ute—and their way of life, so the students would have a greater appreciation for Cloyd and the trials and tribulations he experiences as the main character in *Bearstone*. It was also important for my students to understand who the Native Americans were—as a people—centuries ago and what they were left with after the Trail of Tears. Using informational text facilitated this.

FIGURE 35

REFLECTION ON HOW THE IDENTITY OF NATIVE AMERICANS HAS CHANGED OVER TIME

When I was thinking about what to write, I thought about the first thing I learned about Native Americans. They were called Indians then. It was about the first Thanksgiving and how they helped the Pilgrims and celebrated with a big feast. When I thought about that, I thought the Native Americans must have been proud and kind to help the way they did. Then I thought about how they were treated on the Cherokee Trail of Tears, and how Native Americans today live on reservations, but we can live wherever we want. It doesn't seem fair. When I thought about what caused this to happen, it seemed to be all about who has the power. Before the Pilgrims came, the Native Americans had the power, but as time passed, the government took it from them, and when it did, it took control of their lives.

The students exhibited keen interest in learning about the Native Americans. By reading the informational articles, they were able to gain a broader perspective, which they later related to the attitudes and reactions of the characters in *Bearstone*. They also learned that there are many different points of view about topics and that perspectives are influenced by who the author is and what he or she intends us to believe.

Throughout this lesson, I could see that my students were becoming more and more comfortable with critical questioning, which we had first begun examining about six weeks earlier. It was as if they had come to understand that traditional comprehension, which used to be our final goal, is now a springboard for critical analysis.

FINAL THOUGHTS ABOUT *BEARSTONE* AND THE INFORMATIONAL TEXTS In this group of lessons, Belinda seeks to give students a historical understanding of some of the difficult issues Cloyd had to deal with in a fictional account. The juxtaposition of nonfiction websites and the fictional text allows students to understand the historical context in much deeper ways. Just by going deeper into the meanings of fictional text, students are establishing a habit of questioning and wondering about the historical and cultural context. In other books they may begin to question the meaning of events—especially those in cultures with which they may not be too familiar. In addition to this conceptual questioning, Belinda gives students the technical skills needed to use information on the Web. By engaging in such a project several times, students may gain a habit of questioning and, as a result, juxtaposing nonfiction websites and fictional texts.

The pedagogy Belinda uses is also unique. Raising questions that were meant to disrupt common ideas about Native Americans and examining in small- and whole-group settings gave students many opportunities to gather and then process information in a very social setting that most 8th graders probably enjoy. The debates also provide a competitive context which is attractive to some students.

How Exploring Identities Becomes Critical Understanding

The lessons in this chapter demonstrate that a variety of critical literacy strategies can be used to help students explore identities from a critical perspective. In these lessons students reasoned beyond identities forged by characters' relationships with others. Pig Four, the three little pigs' sister, was active, brave, and empowered. The three little brother pigs were afraid, which contrasts with the stereotype of brave men rescuing women. The social identities were contrasted against the stereotypical, disrupting the commonplace. The concluding discussion about what girls and boys can do demonstrated how students can free themselves from society's expectations and redefine gender—boys and girls can do everything!

Students in the second grade class at first claimed that Jack in the story *Jack and the Beanstalk* was a hero. We identify with Jack, the main character, maybe because he looks like us. He's on our side. The giants are the others, the enemy. However, after they defined hero and villain, the students reimagined Jack's identity. To be a hero, one has to do good things and rescue others. Killing and stealing are not good, even when the giant that Jack was stealing from was a villain himself. The giant's wife, in contrast, gave food and was considered by some to be nice. Though we are not sure what implications this kind of reimagining will have when we apply these standards to the playground or to our country, these types of exercises—those that disrupt common understandings and examine different views and sociopolitical relationships—free us up to think about our position with our friends and with others in a new way.

Though both Mary Roehrenbeck and Stephanie Romano worked in fifth grade classrooms thinking about the topic of immigration, each group had different ways of discussing and responding with a critical eye. Mary and her class compared the voices of those who immigrated and those who didn't. How did the identities of the immigrants change in comparison to the identities of those who stayed in their native land? Did those who stayed feel "left out" or "relieved" when they didn't immigrate, as friends and family had? Did those who immigrated have doubts or feel that going back was a failure? Mary's class also discussed the political or power relations, especially between immigrants and the ship captains, border control, and medical examiners. As students defined what it meant to be in a vulnerable, less powerful position (identity) and in a more powerful position (identity), they began to understand the needs of each group. These social aspects of identity are particularly evident only as one explores the identities of both the powerful and vulnerable. After they understood the precarious identity immigrants have, their action step was to make immigrants feel more welcome.

In Stephanie Romano's lesson, students explored an understanding of self as a part of a larger group, the family. We all understand our individual selves as we relate to others in social groups. We are happy, smart, friendly not as individuals in isolation but in comparison with others. The family is a strong influence on our individual selves and the way we relate to others outside the family. Understanding the influence our family has on our identity is a hidden but significant part of understanding who we are in the world. As these fifth grade students share their own family history and listen to the histories of others, their hidden history is taken out in public for examination, just as they come to understand others. Such examinations lead to our understanding of multiple viewpoints and the disruption of the idea that we are just like everyone else. In addition, the attitude of tolerance or even celebration of diversity is an action that may lead some of the students to avoid ethnic stereotyping.

Belinda used questions about the authors' intent to interrogate informational texts from the Web. These texts informed the students' reading of historical and cultural contexts for the novel *Bearstone*. Discussions and debates clarified issues, making the reading of *Bearstone* a complex and profound experience for the students. In challenging the students' prior knowledge of the westward pioneer movement with a Native-American perspective, Belinda disrupted the students' understanding of this historical period. Alternative perspectives about the Trail of Tears and relationships with Native Americans were generated in the discussions, leading to a more complex, multi-voiced understanding of the events. The power relationships studied by the students may allow students to transfer their knowledge of this historical situation to present and future representations of other ethnic groups with which Americans may find themselves in conflict.

In the next chapter, we explore Seeing Beyond the Bias. In that theme, students try other ways of imagining and creating different texts to see how their thoughts shake up our understanding of what is normal and how we might think differently.

CHAPTER 5

Seeing Beyond the Bias

◆————————————————————◆

"My students and I often engage in inquiry-based learning, so they question naturally. Still, they were very surprised that they could question the author and information contained in a text. I think now that they understand the possibilities, they will view an increasing number of texts and situations from a critical stance. It's almost as if it's added a new dimension to their thinking abilities."

MARY ROEHRENBECK, sixth grade teacher

As Mary notes, inquiry is a valued component of reading from a critical stance. When we try to discover the bias in text and see beyond it, we use inquiry to critically evaluate the text in its natural complexity. We disrupt commonplace understandings and examine bias and power relationships between people, often by looking at an issue from multiple perspectives. Most of us are familiar with this technique in nonacademic contexts. For example, television news hosts invite people on different sides of an issue to debate each other. Also, newspapers pose a question to different experts and ask them to write in support of it or in opposition to it.

In this chapter, we critically examine texts so we can identify their biases and see beyond them. We begin by discussing the multifaceted nature of reality. Next, we share teacher-authored critical literacy lessons at the primary, intermediate, and middle school levels. Finally, we reflect on seeing beyond the bias when we read from a critical stance.

The Biased Nature of Texts

Proponents of critical literacy claim that all texts are biased to some degree because they can only tell one story or a limited range of stories. Emphasizing or foregrounding that story makes them biased. Consequently, bias is a normal, unavoidable part of expression.

It is the job of the reader to understand the bias and decide how to balance it with their own knowledge. One way we can do this when reading narrative texts is to critically evaluate the perspective the author is representing and then focus on the alternative perspectives of other characters. These alternative perspectives allow the reader to disrupt the bias and insert an alternative viewpoint. For example, when reading *Snow White*, we might view the story from the alternative perspective of one of the seven dwarfs, or when reading *Hatchet*, we might view the story from the perspective of Brian's mother or father. When reading informational text, we can critically evaluate the perspective the author is focusing on and then examine the alternative perspectives of others involved in the historical moment or modern-day occurrence. For example, when reading the story of Rosa Parks, we might view that historical occurrence from the perspective of another passenger on the bus, the bus driver, or a member of Rosa Parks's family. Similarly, when reading *John Adams*, the biography by David McCullough, we might view the text from the perspective of Abigail Adams or Benjamin Franklin.

In critical literacy, seeing beyond the bias helps us to participate in the power relationship we share with the author because when more than one perspective is presented, all of the perspectives voiced have the power to define reality. As readers, we examine alternative perspectives for the purpose of understanding the complexity of the world or power relationships.

Classroom Lessons in Which Readers See Beyond the Bias

This section features a variety of lessons that critically examine bias at the primary, intermediate and middle school levels. As discussed in Chapter 2, the teachers who designed and taught these lessons used a planning format that focused on engaging, guiding, and extending students' thinking. Each of the lessons is described in the teacher's own words. The narratives include text descriptions and feature examples of student work. Figure 36 provides an overview of the lessons, including the instructional level, text, and critical focus.

FIGURE 36

OVERVIEW OF LESSONS IN THE SEEING BEYOND THE BIAS THEME

LEVEL	TEXT	SEEING BEYOND THE BIAS CRITICAL FOCUS
Primary	*The Three Little Pigs* *The True Story of the 3 Little Pigs!*	Juxtapositioning
Primary	*No, David!*	Alternative Book Alternative Lyrics
Intermediate	*Christopher Columbus* *Encounter*	Alternative Perspectives Thinking Hats
Middle School	"Seventh Grade"	Alternative Texts—Written Mind and Alternative Mind Portraits
Middle School	*Meet Christopher Columbus* *Encounter*	Alternative Perspectives Columbus's Sailors' Diary Entries
Middle School	"Raymond's Run"	Alternative Texts—Written Switching Settings Switching Genders Switching Character Traits

BOOKS: *The True Story of the 3 Little Pigs!*
and the classic *The Three Little Pigs*

TEACHER: Leslie Fisher

GRADE: 1

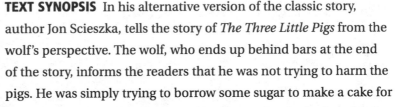

TEXT SYNOPSIS In his alternative version of the classic story, author Jon Scieszka, tells the story of *The Three Little Pigs* from the wolf's perspective. The wolf, who ends up behind bars at the end of the story, informs the readers that he was not trying to harm the pigs. He was simply trying to borrow some sugar to make a cake for his grandmother. He also reports that he had a cold when he visited each pig's home, and it was his powerful sneezes that accidentally knocked down the pigs' houses. The story ends with the wolf in jail, proclaiming his innocence and asking the reader for a cup of sugar.

GETTING STARTED Leslie read aloud the story of *The Three Little Pigs* in the traditional version and compared and contrasted it to Jon Scieszka's transformational fairy tale. In whole-group discussion, students imagined the story being told by other characters whose perspectives would disrupt the story. Then they decided to read more about wolves because they didn't understand what real wolves were like.

ENGAGING STUDENTS' THINKING I began by reading aloud and discussing the original version of *The Three Little Pigs* with the students. We talked about different parts of the story and made personal and text connections. Next, we discussed point of view and focused on the question *Whose viewpoint is expressed?* which I adapted to *Who is telling the story?* We decided that the original story was written from the perspective of the three little pigs.

GUIDING STUDENTS' THINKING Next, we talked about stories that have different versions and are told from different points of view. I explained that I was going to read another book about the three little pigs—*The True Story of the 3 Little Pigs!* I explained that while I was reading, the students should work with partners to think about who was telling the story.

I introduced the story by sharing the cover and title and reading the first few pages. As I finished reading, I prompted students to discuss the story with their partners and think about who was telling the story. When I finished reading, many of the students declared that the story had been told from the wolf's perspective. The remaining students also thought the story had been told from the wolf's perspective, but they didn't think the wolf was telling the truth. This led to quite a discussion and some interesting follow-up activities.

EXTENDING STUDENTS' THINKING To extend their thinking, students orally summarized the wolf's perspective and the pigs'. Next, we discussed other viewpoints from which the story could be written. My question was, "Who else could tell the story?" Some students thought about the pigs' mother's perspective; that prompted a discussion about the wolf's mother and why she isn't in any of the three pigs' stories.

Next, the students wrote a few sentences about a character's perspective. The students' thinking was wide-ranging, and revealed some interesting thought processes. For example, Alex wrote that in both stories "the wolf was very seacky." Alana wrote that in the fairy tales "wolfs are usually bad. In the pig story the wolf was meam." Chris agreed with her. He wrote "the wolf is mean and dascusting." Quanisha thought the wolf was not nice because "the wolf made the little pigs' houses fall down in boph storys." Brian believed the pigs because the wolf was lying. "He was not rily sick. He made it up." Danielle wrote, "I think the wolf BLEW down the pigs' houses. Not sneese them down." Samantha believed the pigs because "pigs are good and wolfs are bad. Wolfs are always bad."

The students' reasoning was diverse, and was often based on both the text and the illustrations. They were happy to share their ideas and freely discussed them. Many of the comments revealed bias against the wolf that led to an interesting discussion of the ways wolves are portrayed in fairy tales. Based on that conversation, we decided that we didn't know enough information about wolves and planned to make *Wolves*, the informational book by Seymour Simon, our next read-aloud.

REFLECTION The students were actively engaged throughout this lesson. They were able to discern at least two perspectives and express their reasoning.

The most interesting outcome of our use of critical questions was the students' discussion of authors writings about wolves and what they want us to believe, and how we need to question what they are writing and examine whether we believe it. During this discussion, Jared asked why the drawings of wolves in stories were so different from photographs of real wolves. That extended our discussion beyond the printed text. We talked about how we could critically read pictures and photographs and what they might tell us. In this case, juxtaposing the wolf's illustrations in *The True Story of the 3 Little Pigs!* and Seymour Simon's photographs of real wolves caused students to observe that the two had very little in common. Differences students noticed included that the wolf in Jon Scieszka's book could talk and acted more like a person than a wolf because he could stand upright and make cakes.

FINAL NOTES ON *THE TRUE STORY OF THE 3 LITTLE PIGS!* AND THE CLASSIC *THE THREE LITTLE PIGS* The first graders in Leslie Fisher's class examined two different perspectives of the three pigs' story. When they examined the two stories side by side, not claiming either to be entirely unbiased, the students saw the situation in a more complex and sophisticated light that resulted in their questioning the authors' thinking. Although the *True Story of the Three Little Pigs!* by Scieszka at first appears to be written from the wolf's perspective, it is in fact a satire on the wolf's perspective that led many of the children not to believe the wolf. Perhaps it is this uneasiness with the characterization of "the wolf's perspective" that led the class to action. Their action was to read an informational text about wolves that would perhaps give the students a better sense of the wolf's perspective. This kind of reflection leading to action that is not completely satisfactory and then reflecting again based on that information is called *praxis* in critical literacy (see Appendix A). Typically, the action leads to some kind of attempt to change an injustice. In this case, students didn't understand the injustice of the wolf's bad reputation, and so their action was continued study leading to an understanding of the wolf's perspective.

CRITICAL LITERACY LESSON

BOOK: *No, David!*
TEACHER: Denise White
GRADE: 2

TEXT SYNOPSIS In the picture book *No, David!* by David Shannon (1998), a boy is shown smiling as he seeks to do things his mother apparently does not allow him to do—she says, "No, David!" The class had already practiced Problem Posing, asking whose voice was in the text and whose was missing. In this section, Denise encourages her students to take an alternative perspective and extend the strategy by writing an alternative text.

GETTING STARTED Denise continued to help her class critically analyze *No, David!*, a book the class has heard her read many times. They reviewed the story and then Denise played devil's advocate by calling one of the characters a "troublemaker." The students defended that character and wrote in their journals. Then, in a whole-group and afterward a small-group discussion, students tried to explore the perspective of another character in the story. They drew captioned pictures and shared their findings. Afterward, they wrote new lyrics to a familiar song, reflecting their new thoughts.

ENGAGING STUDENTS' THINKING I engaged the students by having a whole-group discussion about our previous day's lesson when we had used *No, David!* to learn how to use Problem Posing. Today we would use the same book to learn about Alternative Perspectives.

GUIDING STUDENTS' THINKING The illustrations in the book *No, David!* are very funny and my students enjoyed laughing at the main character's funny antics. My goal was to have students think about David's actions and consider his thoughts and feelings from his viewpoint. After our review I began the discussion with my opinion of the main character, David.

Denise:	I think David is a troublemaker. He never listens to his mom and always makes a mess. David is a bad kid, and I'm sure glad he's not in this class.
Students:	David isn't bad, he doesn't know anything. Yeah, maybe he's in preschool. Maybe he's only 4 years old.
Denise:	You mean David is not trying to dump the fish out of the bowl or break the dishes on the shelf?
Students:	No, he wants to help his mom feed the fish. He only wants a cookie. He's hungry. He wants a snack.

During the discussion, the students became defenders of David's actions. They quickly made personal connections to David and were able not only to see things from his point of view but also connect it to their own lives. After our discussion, students wrote in their response journals. They chose an illustration from the book and wrote about it from David's point of view. I wanted to know what they thought David was thinking and why. The students worked in small groups during this activity. They first chose their favorite illustration and shared with the group what they thought David was thinking. After their small-group discussions, students responded in their journals.

The next day, we again met for a whole-group discussion, but this time it was to look at the book from David's mother's point of view. I began the discussion with the idea that maybe David's mother was mean but concerned about David's safety. Using the same procedure as the day before, students worked in small groups to share their ideas and respond in their reading journals.

The students were able to look at the book and discuss it from the different characters' perspectives. They were eager to defend David because he was not a bad kid; he only made some bad choices. They were also able to sympathize with the mother, noting her concern for David's safety or that he might make a mess she would have to clean up. As I listened to the small-group discussions, I found that the students were looking at the illustrations as if they were seeing them for the first time. Discussing and responding to the book from different perspectives helped them to see the book in a completely different way.

FIGURE 37

FIGURE 38

EXTENDING STUDENTS' THINKING

With the idea of creating an alternative text, we decided to make a class book to which each student contributed one page. The class discussed ways it could rewrite the text. Many of the students began to focus on what David could do instead of climbing on a chair or jumping on the bed. The final decision was to create a book of "yes" activities for David, so the title of our book would be *Yes, David!* We brainstormed a list of ideas that I wrote on chart paper. The students were eager to create a book where David was told "yes" instead of "no." Figures 37 and 38 show examples of the students' work.

The second alternative text that the class created was a song. We did this in a whole group. I asked the students if they knew the song "Twinkle, Twinkle, Little Star." The class immediately began singing the song, showing that they were quite familiar with it. I explained to them that we would change the song title to "David, David" instead of "Twinkle, Twinkle" and write song lyrics that would reflect the mother's perspective. At that point, one of the students suggested we change it to "Davey, Davey." A vote was taken and the first two words were changed. As the class worked on the song they quickly realized that some of the words would need to rhyme in order for it to sound right. Once students were able to brainstorm some rhyming words and "Twinkle, Twinkle, Little Star" was sung many times, we knew the melody and how the new lyrics were working. In the end, the class was able to write lyrics that everyone was satisfied with. The finished song was:

Davey, Davey, Little Boy

Davey, Davey, little boy.

Please pick up all of your toys,

Be like an angel in the sky,

Listen to your mother and don't make her cry.

Davey, Davey, lil Ile boy,

Please pick up all of your toys.

REFLECTION As I reflect on this past week, I feel that I have learned as much from this experience as my students have. I observed my students working together and sharing their ideas about the illustrations and characters. It was exciting to see their thinking move beyond the obvious and respond to what was not said or shown in the text. There were times when I was concerned that certain students did not understand or seemed confused, but in time—and through explanation and modeling—all students were able to participate. It was also exciting to see students thinking about their responses even when we were not discussing them. Several came up with ideas for the book or song lyrics later in the day, when we were doing math or coming in from recess.

I also learned through this experience that these activities are multilevel and meet the needs of all students. Some students enjoyed the group discussions while others were able to share their ideas through writing and drawing. As I observed my students becoming more critically aware, I realized that I too was looking at the books we read in class from a different perspective. I felt that the lessons and strategies I taught were very successful. I am looking forward to witnessing the growth and progress of my students as they become more critically aware.

FINAL NOTES ON THE *NO, DAVID!* LESSON In Denise White's class, students took a conceptual leap when they were willing to comprehend the story of *No, David!* by looking beyond and behind the text to see the different perspectives and the concerns of both David and his mother. The ability to identify both views as biased and recognize that each perspective adds a layer of complexity to understanding helped these second graders to see beyond the bias.

CRITICAL LITERACY LESSON

BOOKS: *Christopher Columbus* and *Encounter*
TEACHER: Jennifer Sassaman
GRADE: 5

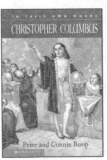 

TEXT SYNOPSIS *Christopher Columbus* recounts the life and times of Columbus. *Encounter* describes Columbus's first visit to the island that was inhabited by the Taino people. It is told from the perspective of a young Taino boy and relates the true—yet often tragic—outcomes of Columbus's exploration.

GETTING STARTED Jennifer used students' prior knowledge and a book about the voyages of Christopher Columbus to engage students and help them to understand Columbus's exploration from one perspective. Next, she asked the students what they knew about perspective and read a book about the arrival of Columbus that was written from the perspective of an island native. Then she asked the students to move beyond the two perspectives they had read and imagine other perspectives on the voyages of Christopher Columbus. Finally, the students brainstormed what those perspectives might have been, became "experts," and shared their thinking.

ENGAGING STUDENTS' THINKING To activate prior knowledge, the students and I used Columbus as our focus and created a semantic map. The students contributed information about his ships, when he sailed, which country he was from, which country he sailed from, and why he was exploring. All of their responses reflected information they had learned about Columbus through their textbooks. To verify the information on our map and provide other facts, I read aloud sections of *Christopher Columbus* by Peter and Connie Roop. The text confirmed students' original thoughts and provided some new information, which we added to the semantic map. When the map was completed, we discussed it and several students noted that we knew a lot about Columbus.

GUIDING STUDENTS' THINKING Next, I asked students to work in small groups to discuss what they thought a person's perspective was. After a brief discussion, one group suggested, "It's how people think," another group said it was "a person's point of view." We continued to discuss perspectives and noted that several people might have different ways of looking at the same topic and that characters in the same story might tell the story in different ways. After we discussed a few examples, I explained that we could also talk about history and events such as Columbus's voyage from different perspectives.

Next, I introduced the students to the book *Encounter* by Jane Yolen and explained that this book was about Columbus's explorations, but it was written from a different perspective. I prompted the students to consider the perspective featured in the story as they read it. Then students engaged in the patterned partner-reading technique of predict–read–discuss (See Chapter 2). As I listened to different groups reading, I heard them making excellent predictions about who the "birds with white teeth" were and what was going to happen to the people in the tribe.

When they finished reading, we discussed that *Encounter* was written from the perspective of a young Taino native, as opposed to the book *Christopher Columbus*, which the students noted was written from Columbus's perspective. We also discussed the similarities and differences between what we had previously known about Columbus and what we had learned from reading the young boy's perspective.

EXTENDING STUDENTS' THINKING Next, we used Jigsaw II, a cooperative learning technique, to facilitate our moving beyond the bias and learning about alternative perspectives. In small groups, the students brainstormed and contributed to a list of the different perspectives that could be considered when talking about Columbus's voyage. The list included those of Columbus, the Tainos, the sailors on Columbus's ships, and King Ferdinand and Queen Isabella of Spain. Then each member of the existing small groups chose a different perspective to assume, and the students regrouped so that everyone who represented a particular view could work together. For example, the student from each of the original small groups who chose to represent Columbus's view moved to a new group comprised only of students working on that perspective. In their new perspective-based groups, students discussed what they knew about that perspective and used research resources, including informational books, such as *The Tainos: The People Who Welcomed Columbus* (Jacobs, 1992) and websites, such as Medieval Sourcebook Christopher Columbus: Extracts from Journal <http://www.fordham.edu/halsall/source/columbus1.html>, Columbus <http://library.thinkquest.org/J002678F/columbus.htm>, and Christopher Columbus <www.biography.com>.

When the students felt they had a good understanding of the perspective they had selected, they returned to their original groups and shared their points of view. Consequently, when these groups met, they had one group member who had become an expert about each of the perspectives. They engaged in discussion from the multiple perspectives and recorded essential information on their Thinking Hats chart (see Figure 39).

Jigsaw II is a cooperative learning technique in which students work in two organized small groups: the original group and the expert group. They begin in their original group, which is often formed heterogeneously. Then they regroup according to a choice they've made—in this case which perspective they wanted to represent. In the expert group they discuss and expand their understanding of their selected topic (in this case the perspective they chose to represent). Finally, they return to their original group, where they present what they learned in the expert group. In this case, each original group would then have one member who had become an expert in each of the brainstormed perspectives. <http://edservices.aea7.k12.ia.us/framework/ strategies/jigsaw.pdf>

After the groups shared their charts, we had a whole-class discussion. First, we discussed Columbus. The students wanted to know why more detailed information about the Tainos wasn't in most textbooks. They wanted to know who decided what went into textbooks. This resulted in a fascinating discussion of the power relationships that exist not only between the reader and the author but among the reader, the author, and the publisher.

Next, we reflected on why it is important when reading not only to consider alternative perspectives but also all possible points of view. In order to make connections to everyday life, I asked the students if there was a topic they could think of that should be considered from multiple perspectives. One student used the example of the war in Iraq and how

FIGURE 39

THINKING HATS

Perspective One: Columbus

- I am proud that I convinced Queen Isabella to give me money for the ships and that I'm in control of them.
- The voyages were my idea, so I should get to keep whatever we find.
- I will be kind to the natives, so they will give me lots of riches. Then I will take some of them as slaves.
- I am worried that my sailors will betray me.

Perspective Two: The Tainos

- We did not know where the sailors came from.
- We welcomed the sailors and gave them gifts.
- We thought they were our friends.
- Columbus betrayed us and took our people as slaves.
- Our lives will never be the same.

Topics in:

Columbus's Voyages

Perspective Three: The Sailors

- It is exciting to be sailing the seas as explorers.
- We should all share anything we find.
- We sailed a long time and were homesick and scared.
- On the final voyage we took control of the ships.

Perspective Four: Queen Isabella

- I am smarter than the other leaders.
- I will give Columbus the money he needs.
- I think Columbus will discover great riches.
- I will become even wealthier when Columbus's voyages are successful.

people might have different thoughts about it if they were soldiers, knew someone who was in the military, or were of Middle Eastern descent. This led to a discussion of all the different perspectives that should be considered. Then another student suggested that we should consider different perspectives even when we just have conversations among ourselves. The other students agreed. That was when I knew my students were on their way to becoming critically aware.

REFLECTION I chose to use the book *Encounter* to discuss alternative perspectives of Columbus's voyage because I knew the students had a lot of standard knowledge about Columbus and I wanted them to see the whole picture. The book worked well, and with guidance and practice the students began to understand alternative perspectives and came up with some very good ideas. Once they were able to put themselves in someone else's shoes, I saw the "light bulbs" begin to turn on and they were genuinely excited about sharing their ideas.

FINAL NOTES ON THE *CHRISTOPHER COLUMBUS* AND *ENCOUNTER* LESSON

By combining social teaching techniques and multiple perspectives, Jennifer Sassaman helped her students understand this important event not from one side or the other side but from a range of perspectives not only concerning Christopher Columbus's arrival in the Americas but also current events, such as the war in Iraq. Students' increasing realization that reality is not simple occurred as Jennifer called on them to problematize their simplistic understanding (see Appendix A). Jennifer found that this multifaceted and complex understanding of the clash of two cultures was not a burden to students but seemed to invigorate them, opening them up to many different, complex, and interesting worlds. This new, complex world disrupts our simplistic, one-version understanding of the world and makes everything more interesting.

BOOK: "Seventh Grade"

TEACHER: Denise Adamoyurka

GRADE: 7

TEXT SYNOPSIS In this short story by Gary Soto, Victor, a 13-year-old boy, is starting his first day of seventh grade. He is excited, yet nervous. Victor is in love with Teresa, another seventh grader, and is convinced that this will be the year that he makes her his girlfriend. Victor embarrasses himself in French class in front of Teresa but, luckily, the French teacher takes pity on Victor and does not embarrass him further. "Seventh Grade" is a humorous story about the trials and tribulations that a young seventh grader experiences as he begins another school year.

GETTING STARTED After engaging the students in the topic by asking students questions (Anticipation Guide) about a historical event, Denise gave examples of perspectives and then invited the class to come up with more perspectives related to that same event. After reading the text and pausing when appropriate to make connections, students created Mind and Alternate Mind Portraits and rewrote the text to anchor their understanding of the different perspectives.

ENGAGING STUDENTS' THINKING Before we started reading the story, we activated background knowledge by completing an Anticipation Guide based on seventh grade school and friend experiences. Ideas included, "Being in seventh grade is exciting," "Sometimes students daydream in class," "Sometimes people act silly around someone they have a crush on," and "I think I will like seventh grade." We discussed responses to each statement and related them to the start of our school year.

Next, we discussed point of view. I used World War II and the bombing of Pearl Harbor as an example. We discussed looking at the war from both the American perspective and the Japanese perspective. Students also thought about looking at the war from a soldier's perspective as well as a civilian's perspective. Next, we previewed our text and made predictions about the story based on the title and the statements in the Anticipation Guide.

GUIDING STUDENTS' THINKING We read the text together by alternating my read-aloud with silent reading. We stopped periodically to discuss the story and make or confirm text-self, text-text, or text-world connections.

Mind Portrait	Alternative Mind Portrait

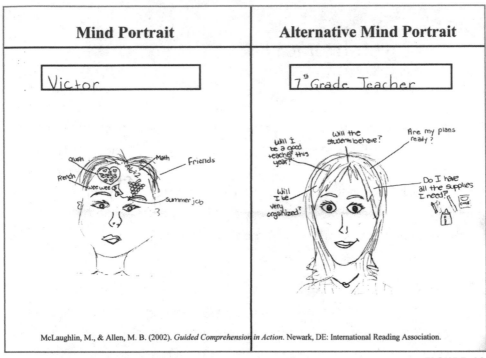

McLaughlin, M., & Allen, M. B. (2002). *Guided Comprehension in Action*. Newark, DE: International Reading Association.

FIGURE 40

EXTENDING STUDENTS' THINKING When we finished reading the text, we discussed rewriting the story from different perspectives. We decided to begin by identifying two perspectives using Mind and Alternative Mind Portraits (McLaughlin & Allen, 2002b) to focus on the perspectives of two different characters. When the portraits were completed, we shared and discussed them in small small groups (see Figure 40). Then the students worked with partners to rewrite "Seventh Grade" from a different perspective.

The students enjoyed reading and hearing each other's stories. A majority of the students wrote from the teacher's perspective. Some of the students wrote stories that sympathized with teachers and the work they do. Others wrote stories about teachers who take aspirin and hope the kids do not misbehave.

REFLECTION I felt that this lesson went very well. The students were active participants during the reading, and they reasoned through the process of looking at the story from another perspective. They also seemed to appreciate the alternative mode of response provided by the Mind and Alternative Mind Portraits (McLaughlin & Allen, 2002b). They came up with some great ideas and had fun working with groups to reimagine and rewrite the story from alternative perspectives.

FINAL NOTES ON THE "SEVENTH GRADE" LESSON For seventh graders to be able to look at seventh grade from the perspective of other students and teachers as a result of reading and discussing a text reflects a broader understanding of texts. In Denise Adamoyurka's class, when they understand the text from these different viewpoints, they disrupt the commonplace routine of reading and responding or reading and replicating the same information.

CRITICAL LITERACY LESSON

BOOK: *Meet Christopher Columbus* and *Encounter*
TEACHER: Susan Sillivan
GRADE: 8—English Language Learners (ELL)

TEXT SYNOPSIS *Meet Christopher Columbus* by James T. DeKay recounts the life and times of Columbus. *Encounter* by Jane Yolen describes Columbus's first visit to the island that was inhabited by the Taino people. It is told from the perspective of a young Taino boy and relates the true—yet often tragic—outcomes of Columbus's exploration.

GETTING STARTED Susan assessed students' prior knowledge about Columbus and then invited students to partner-read a book about Columbus that was written from his perspective. Next, in whole group, the students discussed perspective and wrote a diary from the sailor's perspective. Finally, the students read *Encounter*, which was written from the native perspective and wrote their own books individually from different perspectives.

ENGAGING STUDENTS' THINKING Before reading, I asked the students to consider what they knew or believed about Columbus, his voyages, and the discovery of the New World. We listed responses on the board and briefly discussed each. Next, I introduced the text, *Meet Christopher Columbus*. I explained that we would partner-read approximately half the book, stop to discuss what we had read and react to what we had read, and then continue partner-reading.

GUIDING STUDENTS' THINKING I prompted the students to think about who was telling the story, what they wanted us to believe, and why the story was presented in that way as they read. I also encouraged them to note information that confirmed what we had already discussed about Columbus and information that was new to them.

The students partner-read the first half of the book. They used the Bookmark Technique (see Chapter 2) to note sections of text that they thought included important facts, words they wanted the whole class to talk about, something that confused them, and illustrations that helped them to understand the text. We discussed points that the students thought supported their own knowledge, several references to facts that they had been taught in school, and new information. For example, most did not know that Columbus had made demands of Queen Isabella. This surprised them and made them look at him differently.

Every student agreed the story was told from Columbus's perspective. Several also said that "it was history," indicating to me that they accepted it as being totally factual and without bias.

Our discussion concluded and the students finished partner-reading the story. Then we discussed the information they thought to be important from the second half of the book.

EXTENDING STUDENTS' THINKING I asked the students to think about who else could tell the story of Columbus. They listed the queen, the other ship captains, the people they found on the island, and the sailors on the ships. The students deliberated about how these people might have looked at things differently. Most of the class was interested in the perspective of the sailors on the ship. As a group, we decided that we would write a version of this historic event as a sailor. Since Columbus's journal(s) had played a role in the book, they chose to write using a diary format. We began the diary entries as a group, and then the students completed them individually (see Figure 41).

To further extend their thinking, students had the opportunity to independently read *Encounter*. I introduced the book in class and we discussed some of the similarities and differences between the two books about Columbus. Then students read the book on their own and wrote a version from a different perspective (see Figure 42).

REFLECTION I taught several things during this lesson, but the most important thing students learned was to question what they read—and not believe everything authors write, just because it's history. Most people tend to accept whatever they read ("If it's in print, it must be true"). This is especially true of my students, who are all English-Language Learners. This lesson was challenging for them because it required that they reason at higher thinking levels.

FIGURE 41

EXCERPTS FROM A
STUDENT-AUTHORED SAILOR'S DIARY

September 14, 1492

I am afraid that Columbus has lost his mind and taken us on an impossible journey. He keeps telling us that we will find land, but I don't believe him anymore. We have not seen land in weeks. I don't think anyone has ever sailed this far. When we set sail, I thought this was an adventure, but I am beginning to think that Columbus doesn't know what he is doing. I think we should turn back, before we all die.

September 22, 1492

We are tired and hungry and sick, but we continue to sail. The ocean seems endless. I don't think we will ever find land. I think we're going to die on the sea. I used to think the ocean was beautiful and it was fun to be exploring. Now I think we will die here and never see our families again.

October 12, 1492

I cannot believe it! Columbus was right! Today we landed on an island. It felt so good to be off the ship and on the ground. We were met by island natives. They didn't speak our language and we didn't speak theirs, but they were still able to welcome us. We exchanged gifts and explored the island. We were all very happy to reach land and have fresh water. We are looking for riches on the island to take home with us. I wonder if the natives will let us take them.

FIGURE 42

THE STORY OF *ENCOUNTER*
FROM THE CHIEF'S PERSPECTIVE

That morning I saw three gigantic ships approaching our island. When I first saw them, I didn't know what they were or where they came from. I had a bad feeling. I didn't know if they were gods or humans. I didn't know, and even though I was the chief of the tribe, I was scared.

When they reached the shore, I could see that they were people. I welcomed them and offered them gifts. They gave me gifts, too. Then one of the children in our tribe bothered me. He said, "Don't welcome them! Don't welcome them!" But I didn't listen. No one listened. That night we all had a feast. Again the young boy warned me, but I didn't listen.

When the sailors were leaving, they took many things from our island and some of our people, including the young boy who had tried to warn us. He seemed scared. Before the ships had traveled too far, he jumped off and swam back to shore. Then he told me how the other members of the tribe that had been taken had been tied up and thrown into the bottom of the ship. He said they would become slaves and never be free again. I wished I had listened to him when he tried to warn me.

I was especially interested in teaching a lesson that incorporated these texts because my students are all Latinos, the direct result of this interaction between cultures. I thought it was extremely important for them to understand that the European perspective is not the only perspective. It was also interesting to note that a number of the students did not know that their language was originally European.

FINAL NOTES ON *MEET CHRISTOPHER COLUMBUS* AND *ENCOUNTER* Susan Sillivan's class not only compared and contrasted two different texts but also critically examined characters to see how the sailors, the queen, Christopher Columbus, and the natives might have described the events. The discussions surrounding the readings were followed up by writing simulated diary entries and alternative versions of the stories. This questioning of the text and attempting to see the whole situation of the voyage beyond the limits of the words in the book makes the reader understand in a multifaceted way. It also allows students to examine power relationships between the different people involved in that historical event.

CRITICAL LITERACY LESSON

BOOK: "Raymond's Run"

TEACHER: Kathy Franson

GRADE: 8

TEXT SYNOPSIS "Raymond's Run," a short story by Toni Cade Bambara, is about Squeaky, a teenage black girl growing up in Harlem whose job it is to take care of her disabled brother Raymond. Although at first she tries to focus on advancing herself by beating people in running races and in arguments, later she finds that coaching Raymond to run and win races and making friends is more satisfying. In this lesson, Kathy Franson engages, guides, and extends her students' learning as they imagine what that story might look like in an alternative setting.

GETTING STARTED Kathy engaged and guided students in the literal understanding of a short story through pair sharing and whole-group discussions. Critical questions were posed in pairs and whole group to see how the story might be different if they were to switch the genders, settings, and character traits (see Chapter 2).

ENGAGING STUDENTS' THINKING Since the story was about personal growth and taking care of others, I asked students, in pair sharing and whole-group discussions, to think about times when they were asked to take care of others and times when they felt they experienced personal growth. They shared their thoughts with a partner, and we briefly discussed them as a class. Then I introduced "Raymond's Run."

GUIDING STUDENTS' THINKING During reading, the students reflected occasionally on the ideas of the text and the vocabulary, and marked words that helped them visualize the characters. I also monitored the students' reading to make sure they understood the story. After reading, class discussion focused on plot lines and on the growth that occurred in the character, Squeaky, when she came to think more about her brother's well-being than her own. Students also wrote down their thoughts about the conflict in the story and their own connections with disabled people.

EXTENDING STUDENTS' THINKING Next, the critical questions were posed in pairs and whole-group discussions. We focused mostly on alternative texts that might change the story in some way and help shake up the meaning of the text. Students then rewrote or reillustrated parts of the story and presented their alternative thoughts to the class. The following are the directions for the "Raymond's Run" Response Project:

> **Choose one of the following options to complete and present to the class on Thursday:**
>
> 1. Select an event from the story. Write and perform an alternative version of the event. Be sure to include dialogue for you and your partner to perform.
>
> 2. Create two illustrations. One should illustrate the setting from "Raymond's Run" and one should illustrate an alternative setting. Write a paragraph describing how the alternative setting would affect the plot.
>
> 3. Select a published story that would be a good alternative text. Write an essay explaining why that story is an alternative text.

Students' responses were very creative. One student wrote an alternative story about what would happen if the story were set in a well-to-do neighborhood (Setting Switch; see Chapter 2). It showed Squeaky, the main character, having to spend more time working with her brother versus well-to-do Squeaky being able to devote more of her time to her passion, running. It is often the case that while some poorer students are expected to

FIGURE 43

spend extra time helping out at home, other, more well-to-do children are freer to explore their goals. Of course, the rich Squeaky could choose to take care of Raymond, but the point is that, as a well-to-do person, she would have a choice. A discussion of how being rich can provide choices keeps students from romanticizing how great it was that Squeaky took care of her brother. Students thereby avoid celebrating the joys of poverty and a resultant justification or even glorification of an unequal society. Figure 43 shows a PowerPoint slide of Squeaky in well-to-do surroundings.

Other students switched the gender roles (Gender Switch; see Chapter 2), making Raymond the caregiver and Squeaky the mentally slower sister. This perspective allows us to see men in a kind and giving role that is stereotypically reserved for women. Again, this activity, by switching the gender roles, disrupts the stereotype and provides the critical reader with a different perspective.

Another alternative perspective students created traded in Squeaky as a hard-running tomboy for a girl who likes ballet instead (Personality Switch; see Chapter 2). Perhaps Raymond likes ballet as well and gains Squeaky's affection by dancing, instead of running. Seeing the two of them dancing ballet might disrupt commonplace concepts.

REFLECTION I believe there were some very positive outcomes of this lesson. First, it encouraged the students to think. They seemed uncomfortable as we worked on this, and they wanted to run to me for answers. Perhaps because this was a fairly new strategy for me, I encouraged them to come up with their own answers. And they did.

The second positive outcome was that the students had an opportunity to be creative. I received a variety of responses, from short play scripts to animated PowerPoint presentations to hand drawn pictures. The lesson changed some of the students' ideas about the story, but others' not as much. I am eager to see the depth of understanding these students and I develop by the end of the year through the use of these critical strategies that help us look at texts in different ways.

FINAL NOTES ON THE "RAYMOND'S RUN" LESSON In Kathy Franson's class, students thought about many ways to raise different perspectives about what the story might have looked like in alternative settings or with different characters. By doing this, the story began to take on multiple meanings that extended far beyond literal comprehension.

When Seeing Beyond the Bias Becomes Critical Understanding

These critical literacy lessons concentrate on how readers challenge commonplace meanings by seeing beyond the bias and constructing alternatives to the text the author wrote. In these investigations, students reimagine the story from a different perspective, juxtapose an already familiar competing story and the original text, or simply imagine a different set of circumstances and attitudes. In Leslie Fisher's juxtaposing of the two stories, students appeared to be combative supporters of either the pigs or the wolf. By reading the two stories next to each other, the authority one author has is contested by the other author, who claims to tell the "true" story. This creates space for readers such as those in Leslie's class to explore reasons why one or the other might be true. The teacher invites the readers to explore beyond the bias and be active constructors, using their own reasoning resources. Since no teacher (as the authority) can give a final word on what really happened, the readers feel empowered to make an argument for their perceptions of the story.

In Denise White's *No, David!* lesson, the teacher takes David's perspective one day and then, through discussion, leads the students to understanding the mother's concerns for David's safety (not to tip over the fish bowl) and her own desire for a clean house (when David walks into the house with dirty feet). The class sees how both perspectives have validity without having to decide that one or the other person is right. This thinking demonstrates a level of sophistication that sees beyond the bias of one perspective and far exceeds literal comprehension.

In a similar way in Jennifer Sassaman's fifth grade class and Susan Sillivan's eighth grade class, students who juxtaposed the perspective of the Taino people in *Encounter* and the European perspective in *Meet Christopher Columbus* found that the distance between the perspectives opened up space for even more perspectives. In Jennifer's fifth grade, the idea of different perspectives which were instantiated by the reading of the two texts engaged students personally in the ideas and opened up the possibility of having even more perspectives and sharing them using a jigsaw approach. In Sillivan's eighth grade class, students who appeared to have strong beliefs in the inerrancy of authors, were shaken up and came to recognize the role of bias and perspective in texts.

After reading the short story "Seventh Grade," students in Denise Adamoyurka's class began to explore the different ways in which students and teachers experience the same event. Students seemed intrigued by the teacher perspective and able to sympathize with a perspective other than their own. In Kathy Franson's eighth grade classroom, students reimagined an alternative story in different settings to shake up their understanding of Squeaky's sacrifice in caring for her older brother. They also recast the story, swapping gender roles to see if the story would change at all when boys became girls and vice versa. All of these students looked beyond the bias and created alternative perspectives, opening up questions and issues about what it means to be rich or what it means to be a girl or boy. Again, the contested spaces made students able to explore and wonder about the stories, the society they live in, and how they might rethink their roles in it.

In the next chapter we move beyond classroom accounts of critical literacy lessons and discuss teachers' and students' reflections about critical literacy. We also provide some final thoughts on how critical literacy disrupts our common understanding and opens up new ways for thinking about our lives.

CHAPTER 6

Reading a Whole New World

"Reading from a critical stance has helped my students to think beyond the printed page, value their ideas, and comprehend at deeper, more complex levels."

MATTHEW REKAB, third grade teacher

Earlier in the book, we talked about the importance of viewing reading as a thinking process. In his reflection, Matthew makes connections to this idea, noting that reading from a critical stance has raised the level of students' thinking and encouraged them to reason through and beyond the author's words.

So we have come full circle. We began this book by introducing the theoretical framework of critical literacy. Then, we provided numerous examples of critical literacy in action at a variety of grade levels. Now it is time for you to continue developing your personal understanding of critical literacy so you can begin to infuse it in your teaching.

In this, our final chapter, we continue to support your journey to critical awareness by sharing reflections from the teachers and students with whom we have been working. We begin by delineating the teachers' thoughts. Then we share reflections from students at a variety of grade levels. Finally, we discuss our thoughts about critical literacy, including our hopes for the future.

The Teachers' Reflections

When we asked teachers to reflect and comment on their critical literacy experiences, they noted that beginning to read from a critical perspective had opened them and their students to experiencing texts (books, articles, films, everyday situations) in a new way. They also noted that, over time, they felt increasingly aware of their—and their students'—ability to think from a critical perspective. A majority of the teachers also commented on a newfound aspect of the student-teacher relationship—one of being partners in critical exploration. Finally, most teachers noted that they perceived themselves as being at the beginning stages of critical awareness—a process that would continue to grow and change over time. (Excerpts from the teachers' reflections can be found at the start of each chapter.)

The Students' Perspectives

When we asked the students what they had learned from their initial experiences with critical literacy, their responses were insightful. Many of them reported that they enjoyed contemplating narrative texts from the perspectives of different characters. When reading informational text, a majority of the students indicated that they previously had been unaware that people make choices about what topics will be included in or excluded from textbooks, and that people make choices about how much of the truth will be included in texts. Many cited their ability to challenge the author and the text as the most valuable outcomes of their critical literacy experiences.

When we discussed reading from a critical perspective with the primary students, most of their reactions dealt with examining different perspectives in narrative text. Fairy tales written from perspectives other than the original version, such as *The Fourth Little Pig*, *The Three Little Wolves and the Big Bad Pig*, and *The True Story of the 3 Little Pigs!*, contributed to students' understanding that stories could be told from different points of view. When the students read informational text from a critical perspective, they seemed most comfortable—and logically so—when they were reading on topics about which they had a lot of background knowledge. "Animals" was one such topic. For example, when reading Seymour Simon's *Wolves*, the students were thoroughly intrigued by the impressive photographs that illustrate the text. By viewing and discussing them from a critical perspective, students learned that, in addition to text, photographs and illustrations can be "read" from a critical stance. Through this book, the students learned about the different kinds of wolves, where they live, what they do, and other factual information. But then they wanted to talk about wolves and their community, why people don't have wolves for pets, and why wolves sometimes harm people. That discussion caused the students to begin reading information about what people have done to wolves—how much of what used to be the wolves' wilderness has been turned into our cities and housing developments. That, in turn, caused the students to question what they could do to help animals—if not the wolves, then animals living in their community.

Students at the intermediate and middle school levels also reflected on what they had learned in the beginning stages of their critical literacy experiences. In addition to discussions, they kept reflective journals. Excerpts from their journals, in their own words, follow:

It's interesting to read what's in the book and then think about what is missing or not talked about much. I wonder how many people don't know there's more to know than what the book says. **—JOSEPH**

People think different ways and authors are people, so they think their ways. They write what they want us to know. We need to see what else there is. **—CODY**

I learned that someone could be standing right next to you and could be seeing something totally different. They could think different than I do. I never thought about that before. **—DENISE**

I learned that if you ask, "What does the author want us to think?" it makes you think about that and what else there is that might not be in the book. You can think about how other characters would tell the story or how other people would talk about what happened in history. **—AMI**

It's like the information used to be in the book and now the information is there and everywhere else. **—DIANE**

I learned that if you read in a critical way you learn more. It gives you more than one way to look at something. It works in school and it works outside of school, too. —**DAVID**

I learned that there's more to know than just what's printed on the page. —**JOSEF**

I learned we should always think and not just accept what's in the book or what we're told. —**DANIEL**

I learned that there might be other things to know about what I'm reading that I won't know until I think about what's not in the book. —**HEATHER**

I used to just read what was there on the page. Now I do that and then I think about what's not on the page—what the author didn't write. —**KALEENA**

I learned that you don't know something until you think about it in different ways. Like even when you talk to someone and say something you have to think about what they're thinking. —**DUANG**

I learned that trying to get into another person's head is a lot of work. —**BRIANNE**

I learned that there could be a thousand other truths about what I'm reading. —**MARZENE**

I learned that authors want us to think the way they do. —**JEROME**

I learned that it's about seeing in a new way—not just what we're reading but what we talk about and what we do. —**ALICE**

As you can see from their reflections, the students expressed their ideas better than we ever could. So we will simply add that they enthusiastically engaged in critical literacy, and that inspired both their teachers and us.

Our Final Thoughts

For us, writing this book has been an experience that has linked the past to the present and the future. Many years ago, when we first read the work of Paulo Freire, we realized the importance of critical literacy—of reading the word and reading the world—of seeing beyond the text, of comprehending at deeper, more complex levels. Our recent work with teachers and students in schools across the country has reaffirmed those beliefs and encouraged us in our quest to make critical literacy accessible. And that brings us to this book, an introductory volume that we hope will help both teachers and students to expand their reasoning, deepen their understanding, and become active thinkers who comprehend from a critical stance.

As teachers, we have always engaged in what Paulo Freire (1970) calls *praxis*: taking action, reflecting, and taking renewed, transformed action. We are educators, and as such, we are never really finished learning. We never stop striving to transform ourselves and our teaching. So, although this book is at its end, our critical awareness—this innovative, expanded way of comprehending beyond the written word—is just beginning, opening us as readers to a new world of exploration and discovery.

Participating in that world, one in which we naturally engage in reflection, action, and transformation, will help us to better understand the global and immediate society in which we live. Like Dorothy when she went to meet the great and powerful Wizard of Oz, we must be able to look behind the curtain to see who is controlling the messages and glitzy images we encounter every day. This definition of the reading act repositions us as researchers and language analysts and calls upon us to be open to the possibilities of comprehending with a critical edge as we create our own roads to critical understanding.

Appendix A: Glossary of Critical Literacy Terms

Banking Model of Education
According to Freire (1970), in the banking model of education teachers view students as bank accounts into which they, the teachers, deposit facts and withdraw information when tests are given. A similar metaphor is that students are containers that teachers fill up with facts. Because the facts imparted do not seem to relate in any way to the students' lives, students don't usually use "the deposits." In such models, students are viewed as objects to be acted upon rather than as participatory subjects who make decisions about how and what they learn.

Bias Bias is a partiality or favoritism toward one perspective or another. Proponents of critical literacy claim that all texts have bias to some degree because they tell only one story or a limited range of stories. Emphasizing or foregrounding that story makes them biased. Consequently, bias is a normal, unavoidable part of expression. It is the readers' job to understand the bias and decide how to balance it with their own knowledge.

Critical Discourse Analysis In contrast to other types of text analysis, critical discourse analysis examines the purpose and production of the text in the setting in which the text is used. The mere comprehension of an idea when it is isolated from the other words or the context is not sufficient to understand how the text works (Gee, 2000). Those using critical discourse analysis work toward the goals of democracy, equality, freedom, and justice.

Critical Literacy Critical literacy is not a teaching method but a way of thinking and a way of being that challenges texts and life as we know it. Critical literacy focuses on issues of power and promotes reflection, transfor-

mation, and action. It encourages readers to be active participants in the reading process: to question, to dispute, and to examine power relations (Freire, 1970).

Critical Literacy Strategies Critical literacy strategies provide a plan or starting point for helping readers investigate text from a critical perspective. Such strategies include Problem Posing (Wink, 2000), Juxtapositioning, Problematizing (Leistyna, Woodrum, & Sherblom, 1995), Clever Close (AATE & ALEA, 2002), and Alternative Perspectives. Examples of several of these strategies can be found in the lessons in Chapters 3, 4, and 5 of this volume.

Identity Identity is not a set of psychological traits, but rather a process of construction in which perspective, context, and culture play roles (McCarthy & Moje, 2002). Readers' understanding of identity may, in part, emerge through representations in literature. For example, readers may learn that those identified as kings and generals are important, if that is what the text they are reading emphasizes. Conversely, they may learn that midwives or slaves are unimportant if there is limited text devoted to those identities. Readers can also learn about identity through fairy tales. For example, in the traditional fairy tale, *Little Red Riding Hood*, students learn that the females (Little Red and Grandma) are passive victims and the males (the wolf and the woodsman) are active and aggressive. After reading such books, readers may come to identify with the characters in the books.

Naming When a particular perspective is not represented, a reader can name the silenced voice. By raising an issue or perspective that is normally unnoticed, the reader "names" the perspective that previously was silent and brings it to people's attention. Naming then creates opportunities for dialogue, reflection, transformation, and action (Wink, 2000). For example, the words we use are a sign of our biases. In *Harry Potter and the Prisoner of Azkaban*, the overweight Dudley "waddles," not "walks." *Our* armies "take out" or "suppress" while enemy forces "kill" (Janks, 1993). In all of literacy, we seek the power to represent the world—to name it (Shannon, 2001). Advocates of critical literacy suggest that it is only fair that people be able to name their own reality: use their own words to describe their own world.

Positioning and Repositioning

Positioning involves placing readers in contexts that force them to think about themselves in certain ways—for example, thinking that girls do certain types of things and boys do different types of thing (Vasquez, 2003). To help readers not view themselves and those in the text as positioned, they can imagine alternative situations in which the roles are different. Authors can also position readers as consumers of the product in an advertisement or as board members of a corporation participating in a business meeting by giving sales information about the different products sold.

Power   Power in critical literacy is usually put in a social context (i.e., between people). People have power over others. Those with power establish the rules or set the agenda. People with power have their words heard and are followed by the group; those without power have their words ignored. In a school, power relationships are well established, with the principal having the most power, followed by teachers, then parents and, finally, students (Vasquez, 2003). In texts and the discussions that surround them, the author has power to name and describe the event in the story. Teachers can maintain the power of the author by limiting the discussion of texts to the simple summarizing of the ideas in the

text, or the teacher can encourage the students to use their power to rename or reimagine the event in different ways. Traditionally in reading, the emphasis has been on the author's power, but in critical literacy, readers who are text critics actively exert their power by questioning the author's message and its hidden implications.

Praxis   *Praxis* refers to the dialectical approach of reflecting on teaching and the action the learner takes as a result of the teaching (Freire, 1970). Critical theorists believe that learning should serve to transform the classroom, the community, and the world into something more just. So instead of keeping "banked" information on deposit, readers should use it to do good. Of course, doing good can mean many different things. Examples include changing an unjust school policy, writing to a representative about a law that impacts schools in a negative way, acquiring books for the school or community library that represent different views on a particular topic, boycotting a company that has unfair labor practices, or writing and distributing information about conflict management to friends and family. Based on reflection of how such actions create a more just world, the person may shift, add to, or change the action steps to transform the world. Then, upon reflecting on how effective the transformation was, the reader may continue to make changes.

Problematizing   In order to view a situation that appears to be simple in more sophisticated and complex ways, one must problematize, or question, the situation. To problematize, one asks lots of questions about the topic to understand the underlying reasons for the idea or to analyze how the text is constructed. For example, Barbara Comber (2001) observed a teacher who has changed the way she talks about text to her 5- to 8-year-old students, ignoring the obvious questions, such as thinking about the story or about their favorite character, and encouraging students to ask about how the author or illustrator constructed the text. For example, she asked, "What do writers say about girls, boys, mothers, and fathers in the books you read? If you knew the families only by reading the book, what would you say the mother does?" To problematize, the questioner avoids the "obvious" to take notice of the implicit assumptions on which the question or statement is founded.

Reading the World Reading the world means looking behind, around, through, and beyond the information presented in the text. It means to analyze the ideas the text is promoting as well as those it is ignoring, discounting, or marginalizing. Reading the world helps readers understand the author's underlying purpose, so they won't be manipulated by the text (Freire, 1970).

Seeing Beyond the Text Seeing beyond the text means to disrupt the topic—to see it from the perspectives of characters whose views and thoughts are not well represented or from the perspective of characters that are not present in the text. Seeing beyond the text is connected with the critical-literacy phrase, "Read the word; read the world." Reading the word is literal comprehension and reading the world is seeing beyond the text.

Social Constructivist Theory Social constructivism is a theory about knowledge and learning in which learning is understood as "a self-regulated process of resolving inner cognitive conflicts that often become apparent through concrete experience, collaborative discourse, and reflection" (Brooks & Brooks, 1993, p.vii). Meaning is constructed through teacher and student interaction with each other and with texts—including books and media (Au, 1998).

Social Justice or Social Action These terms refer to a sense of fairness between people. In critical literacy, people not only read and have thoughts about what is fair; they also act and seek to act in ways that would promote fairness. This is a moral imperative that people who act on critical thoughts support (Edelsky, 1999). For example, taking social action may mean avoiding buying products from companies who treat their workers unfairly or it may mean e-mailing friends to tell them not to buy from that company. Social action can also be very personal. For example, students who usually argue a lot with classmates could learn about taking another perspective. Later, when they find themselves in a dispute, they could employ social action by thinking about what their classmate's perspective is and restating it to that person to demonstrate empathy with the other person's argument.

Appendix B: Trade Books to Use When Teaching Critical Literacy

In this annotated bibliography we have included titles that we often use when teaching critical literacy. The trade books are listed in one of three categories, although many of them can be used across categories. The first list contains titles that disrupt the commonplace, offer insights into identities, and provide multiple viewpoints. These books problematize (see Appendix A) stereotypical views, opening up a complex world and the possibility of analyzing many different relationships. The second category focuses more strongly on how individuals and groups of people relate to each other because of their ethnic or political affiliations. The third list includes books about people who took action to make a difference in their own lives, in the lives of strangers, or in their communities.

CATEGORY ONE:
Books that Disrupt the Commonplace, Offer Insights into Identities, and Provide Multiple Viewpoints

Adler, D. A. (2003). *Mama Played Baseball*. New York: Gulliver Books.
While Amy's dad is fighting in World War II, her mother gets a job playing baseball on a women's professional team. The story is told from Amy's perspective. Historical background is provided in a note from the author.

Angelou, M. (1998). *Life Doesn't Frighten Me*. New York: Stewart, Tabori & Chang.
Former poet laureate Maya Angelou proclaims that life doesn't frighten her, but she always seems to be looking over her shoulder because the pictures by Jean-Michel Basquiat have a naïve, raw, and edgy feeling to them. It seems that the tone of the text and that of the pictures are so different that the volume embodies two different perspectives.

Atkin, S. B. (2000). *Voices from the Fields: Children of Migrant Farm Workers Tell Their Stories*. New York: Little, Brown.
In this volume, migrant children tell the moving stories of their everyday lives.

Avi. (2002). *Crispin: The Cross of Lead*. New York: Hyperion.
This work of historical fiction chronicles the adventures of Crispin, who loses everything after his mother dies and he is falsely accused of murder. The book details both the boy's discovery of his true identity and the realities of medieval life.

Bauer, M. (Ed.) (1994). *Am I Blue? Coming Out from the Silence*. New York: HarperCollins.
Lois Lowry, Jacqueline Woodson, and other authors provide the reader with a range of views on youth relationships from self-discovery to homophobia, friendship to estrangement. These tough but honest views are controversial and will raise some important issues for discussion.

Bishop, G. (1989). *The Three Little Pigs.* **New York: Scholastic.**
Any caricature of a familiar tale will disrupt the commonplace understanding of the story and add new viewpoints to the characters. In this story, Mrs. Pig dresses in sunglasses and shorts, mowing the lawn while her sons loll by the pool. The wolf dresses in a snazzy warm-up jacket and wears a Walkman.

Brokaw, T. (1998). *The Greatest Generation.* **New York: Greenwillow.**
This volume chronicles World War II through a cross-section of the personal experiences of a variety of men and women, from ordinary people to heroes.

Carroll, A. (Ed.). (2001). *War Letters: Extraordinary Correspondence from American Wars.* **New York: Scribner.**
This collection of 150 letters, which, along with others, constitutes what Carroll describes as "the first, unfiltered drafts of history," spans 130 years of America's involvement in warfare from the Civil War to Bosnia.

Celsi, T. (1990). *The Fourth Little Pig.* **Austin, TX: Steck Vaughn Company.**
Their sister, Pig Four, persuades the Three Little Pigs to overcome their fears of the wolf and go out and live their lives.

Choi, Y. (2001). *The Name Jar.* **New York: Knopf.**
Unhei moves to the U.S. from Korea and attends a new school. On the way to school, other children on the bus tease her about her name because it is different. When she reaches her classroom and is asked for her name, remembering the bus incident, she tells her peers that she hasn't decided on one. Unhei's classmates decide to write suggestions for a name and place it in a "name jar." In the end, she realizes the meaning of her name and decides to use her own name.

Cole, J. The Magic School Bus series. New York: Scholastic.
There are several voices in each of these information-packed books. The children's voices and commentary run alongside the narrative story, which is punctuated with facts about the topic studied. The different perspectives of the children on the school bus are evident.

Creech, S. (1996). *Walk Two Moons.* **New York: Harper Trophy.**
Sal, a thirteen-year-old girl, struggles to understand her mother's sudden disappearance. Sal and her grandparents decide to go on a trip to find her mother. During their travels, Sal tells her grandparents a story about her friend Phoebe, whose mother also left home. In reality, the story of Phoebe turns out to be the story of Sal.

Cruz, B. (2001). *Multiethnic Teens and Cultural Identity.* **Berkeley Heights, NJ: Enslow Publishers.**
This book discusses the many issues facing teens of multiethnic descent, including discrimination and the search for ethnic identity.

Curtis, C. (1999). *Bud, Not Buddy.* **New York: Yearling.**
Bud is tired of living in cruel foster homes and decides to run away. Bud's mission is to find a big-band leader whom he believes to be his biological father.

Curtis, C. (1997). *The Watsons Go to Birmingham—1963.* **New York: Yearling.**
This is the story of an African-American family and their trip to Birmingham to rehabilitate Byron, a troublemaking teenager. The story is told through the eyes of Kenny, Byron's ten-year-old brother, who tells about the family's experiences during the civil rights era.

Erdrich, L. (1999). *The Birchbark House.* New York: Hyperion Books for Children.
Omakayas, a seven-year-old Native-American girl of the Ojibwa tribe, is the only one to avoid the small-pox outbreak on an island in Lake Superior in 1847. This is a true but little known alternative history of the Native Americans. This book would be interesting to pair with *Valley of the Moon* by Sherry Garland, who also writes about Native-American orphans in California in 1845.

Fama, E. (2002). *Overboard.* Chicago: Cricket Books.
Based on a true story, fourteen-year-old expatriate Emily struggles for her life after a ferryboat she is riding on sinks. She saves a Muslim boy by giving him a life jacket and then learns about his faith as they wait to be rescued. This book explains some of the ideas of Islam in a nonthreatening, casual story, providing an alternative perspective on a religion that most Westerners are not acquainted with.

Farris, C.K. (2002). *My Brother Martin: A Sister Remembers Growing up with the Rev. Dr. Martin Luther King, Jr.* New York: Simon and Schuster.
Christine King Farris recounts her memories of her younger brother, Martin, in this biographical and historically informed volume.

Fleischman, P. (1993). *Bull Run.* New York: HarperCollins.
The story of the battle of Bull Run is told from thirteen different perspectives, including those of a general, a slave, the sister of a soldier from Minnesota, and a physician.

Garland, S. (2001). *Valley of the Moon: The Diary of Maria Rosalia de Milagros.* New York: Scholastic.
Much like *The Birchbark House*, this story tells about Maria, whose Native-American family dies of disease after contact with white people. The life and cultural mixture of these two groups is problematized as this period of time is presented as two cultures mixing rather than the cowboy and Indian wars.

Gates, H.L., & West, C. (2000). *The African-American Century: How Black Americans Have Shaped Our Country.* New York: Free Press.
This book focuses on the contributions of black Americans during the twentieth century. It reports and celebrates the multifaceted achievements of African Americans during that one-hundred-year period.

Gay, K. (1995). *I Am Who I Am: Speaking Out About Multiracial Identity.* New York: Franklin Watts.
This book discusses the experiences of adults, youth, and children with biracial or multiracial backgrounds. The author expresses the concerns that biracial and interracial families experience and how society impacts their lives.

Seuss, Dr. (1957). *The Cat in the Hat.* New York: Random House.
Dr. Seuss helps children to see this story from Mother's perspective, which is represented by the fish, as well as from the Cat in the Hat's perspective. At the end, readers are invited to tell what they would say if they had to report on what the children were doing all day.

Geisel, T. (1961). *The Sneetches and Other Stories.* New York: Random House.
Written in typical Dr. Seuss style, "The Sneetches" teaches that prejudice can be costly. Several other stories are included in this volume.

Gold, A.L. (2000). *A Special Fate: Chiune Sugihara, Hero of the Holocaust.* New York: Scholastic.
This biography tells the story of a Japanese diplomat working in Lithuania, who chooses to ignore his orders and listen to his conscience. Despite the risks to himself and his family, Sugihara writes thousands of transit visas and saves the lives of countless Jews.

Gragg, R., ed. (2002). *From the Fields of Fire and Glory: Letters of the Civil War.* San Francisco, CA: Chronicle Books.
This book features 20 letters written by soldiers during the Civil War. It is interactive; the letters, which describe battles, fears, triumphs, and losses, can be removed and read.

Grimes, N. (2002). *Talkin' About Bessie.* New York: Scholastic.
Although poverty, gender discrimination, and racism were obstacles, Bessie Coleman didn't let them stop her from becoming the first African-American female pilot. The book is written in a unique poetry format in which the multiple perspectives of family and friends are presented.

Hoffman, M. (1991). *Amazing Grace.* Glenview, IL: Scott Foresman.
A young girl, who delights in adopting the roles of various famous individuals, is encouraged by her mother and grandmother to pursue and realize her dreams.

Hoyt-Goldsmith, D. (2001). *Celebrating Ramadan.* New York: Holiday House.
This is a warm and thoughtful description of the ways in which a 9-year-old boy from New Jersey celebrates Ramadan with his family. This text disrupts the way most children think of holidays.

Jennings, P., & Brewster, T. (1998). *The Century.* New York: Doubleday.
In this historical volume, the authors report on the accomplishments and everyday experiences of the twentieth century. A special feature is the first-person experiences, individuals who actually witnessed the events report.

Jennings, P., & Brewster, T. (1999). *The Century for Young People.* New York: Doubleday.
This book, a student version of *The Century*, recounts the challenges and dreams of the twentieth century.

Lowell, S. (1992). *The Three Little Javelinas.* Maple City, MI: Rising Moon Books Imprint of Northern Publishing.
In this southwestern version of the Three Little Pigs story, three little javelinas are pursued by a coyote. In this story, a humorous southwestern twist on the original Three Little Pigs, the houses are made of tumbleweed, dried cactus, and adobe.

Macaulay, D. (1990). *Black and White.* Boston, MA: Houghton-Mifflin.
This story is split into four different adjoining illustrated texts, each requiring the reader to construct what is happening in the story and how it relates to the other simultaneously progressing plots and characters.

Maurer, R. (2003). *The Wright Sister.* Brookfield, CT: Roaring Brook Press.
Based on the personal writings of Katherine Wright and the Wright family archives, this volume reveals the sister as an important member of the Wright flying team.

McGhee, A. (2001). *Shadow Baby.* New York: Picador.
Clara, a young girl, chooses an elderly man, Georg, as the focus of her school project. The book recounts Clara's life experiences, including the death of her twin sister, strained family relationships, and her relationship with the illiterate old man.

Mochizuki, K. (1995). *Baseball Saved Us.* New York: Lee and Low.
The Japanese-American Internment is the setting for this story, which recounts a young boy's transition from the life he has known to his time in an internment camp.

Montes, M. (2003). *A Crazy Mixed-Up Spanglish Day.* New York: Scholastic.
Gabi's Puerto Rican heritage makes her whole life an alternative text compared to that of most other young children. This girl lives in two cultures with two languages.

Muñoz Ryan, P. (2000). *Esperanza Rising.*
New York: Scholastic.
During the Great Depression, 14-year-old
Esperanza and her mother move to a labor
camp in California after her father's death.
When her mother becomes ill, Esperanza
works to make enough money to bring her
grandmother to the United States from Mexico.

Na, A. (2003). *Step from Heaven.*
New York: Puffin.
Young Ju, a young Korean girl, and her family
struggle to adjust to life in America, a place
they called heaven when they were back in
Korea. Father becomes disenchanted, angry,
abusive, and eventually alienated from the
family. This book gives us a complex understanding of the immigration experience.

Nam, V. (2001). *Yell-oh Girls! Emerging
Voices Explore Culture, Identity, and
Growing Up Asian American.*
New York: Quill.
Through a collection of personal writings,
young Asian-American girls engage in conversations about the unique challenges they face
in their lives. These essays, poems, and stories
discuss various complex issues. The book
discusses dual identities, culture clashes,
family matters, and self-image from a young
person's perspective.

Olshan, M. (2001). *Finn: A Novel.* **Baltimore,
MD: Bancroft.**
This is a story that problematizes the concept
of parenthood showing how parents can
sometimes be harmful to their own children.
Finn is a retelling of *The Adventures of
Huckleberry Finn*, set in today's world. In this
version, Chloe is kidnapped by her mother
and her mother's boyfriend. Eventually she
escapes and tries to return to her grandparents.

Paterson, K. (1990). *Jacob Have I Loved.*
New York: Harper Trophy.
Caroline and Louise are twin sisters who have
been inseparable for most of their lives.
Caroline is prettier and brighter than Louise

could ever hope to be. Louise's life has seemed
to be full of betrayal and disappointments.
Through her experiences, Louise discovers
that there is a light at the end of the tunnel.

Paterson, K. (1998). *Jip: His Story.*
New York: Puffin.
Jip, an abandoned orphan, is sent to a poor
farm in Vermont because he has no traceable
family to claim him. The farm becomes his
home, where he helps other people with their
lives and develops a friendship with a mysterious man. The mysterious man changes Jip's
life when he helps him learn more about his
identity and how he arrived at the farm.

Pilkey, D. (2001). *Captain Underpants
and the Wrath of the Wicked Wedgie
Woman.* **New York: Scholastic.**
This is a book that is great fun to analyze
critically because it speaks to the concern of
many boys who want to be good-guy heroes,
are still into potty humor, and resent the
control of adults.

Reynolds, P. (1985). *The Agony of Alice.*
New York: Alladin.
Alice's mom passed away many years ago
and she is about to become a teenager. Alice
searches for a beautiful role model who never
makes mistakes. When Alice is placed in the
class of a teacher who is less than perfect,
she is very disappointed but discovers that
being "perfect" and attractive are not the
only things important in life.

Rinaldi, A. (1999). *My Heart Is on the
Ground: The Diary of Nannie Little Rose,
a Sioux Girl, Carlisle Indian School,
Pennsylvania, 1880.* **New York: Scholastic.**
Nannie Little Rose is sent to a government-run
boarding school to learn the white man's
customs and language. She maintains a diary
that details her previous life, a life she will
never forget.

Rowling, J.K. (1998). *Harry Potter and the Sorcerer's Stone.* **New York: Scholastic.**
Harry lives with his mean aunt and uncle and their spoiled son, Dudley. When Harry turns 11, he receives a letter from Hogwarts School of Witchcraft and Wizardry, informing him that he is to report for school. From that day on, his life is transformed into a sometimes baffling, never boring adventure.

Sachar, L. (1993). *Marvin Redpost: Is He a Girl?* **New York: Random House.**
Casey Happleton, Marvin Redpost's friend, has convinced Marvin that if he kisses his elbow he will turn into a girl. Curious about the opposite sex, Marvin experiments and finds himself confused about his gender.

Salinas-Norman, B. (1998). *The Three Pigs: Nacho, Tito, and Miguel.* **Alameda, CA: Piñata.**
Another perspective on the Three Little Pigs takes place in a spicy Southwestern setting where the pigs cook green chile stew and dress in zoot suits, cowboy hats, and guayaberas.

Scieszka, J. (1989). *The True Story of the 3 Little Pigs!* **New York: Penguin.**
Alexander T. Wolf is so upset with the original story of the Three Little Pigs that he vows to set the story straight. In his version of the story, he explains that he just needed to borrow some sugar to bake a cake for his grandmother, but he had a cold and, unfortunately, when he sneezed, the pigs' houses fell down.

Shihab Nye, N. (1999). *Habibi.* **New York: Simon Pulse.**
Liyana and her contemporary Arab-American family move back to Jerusalem. The culture shock is overwhelming for Liyana, especially when she falls in love with a Jewish boy.

Silverstein, S. (1964). *The Giving Tree.* **New York: Harper & Row.**
This story strongly takes the perspective of the happy but sacrificing mother who never gets any thanks from her children. It discounts the perspective of grateful children.

Tchana, K. (2002). *Sense Pass King: A Story from Cameroon.* **New York: Holiday House.**
In this beautifully illustrated story, Ma'antah continually outsmarts the king—not by tricking him in the way that many folktales show, but by being smarter. Here the value of being smart and creative is raised in contrast to tales in which intelligence appears devious and dishonest.

Thomas, V.M. (1997). *Lest We Forget: The Passage from Africa to Slavery and Emancipation: A Three-Dimensional Interactive Book with Photographs and Documents from the Black Holocaust Exhibit.* **New York: Crown Publishing.**
This volume contains information about African-American slavery as compiled in the Black Holocaust Exhibit. It provides truthful historical accounts of the passage from Africa and of working on plantations.

Trivizas, E. (1993). *The Three Little Wolves and the Big Bad Pig.* **New York: Margaret K. McElderry Books, Macmillan Publishing Company.**
In this transformation of the traditional story of the Three Little Pigs, a mother wolf sends her children off to live their lives, warning them to beware of the Big, Bad Pig. They build progressively stronger homes, which the pig destroys. But the last house they build has an unusual effect on the pig, and the story ends with the Three Little Wolves befriending the Big, Bad Pig.

Turner, A. (2003). *Love Thy Neighbor: The Tory Diary of Prudence Emerson, Green Marsh, Massachusetts, 1774.* **New York: Scholastic.**
Prudence tells about her life and the life of her family as they struggle to survive during the American Revolutionary War.

Tuyet, T. (1992). *The Little Weaver of Thai-Yen Village/Co Be Th-Det Lang Thai-Yen.* **San Francisco: Children's Book Press.**

Hien, a young Vietnamese girl, loses her family in the war and is later wounded. Hien must travel to the United States for an operation. After arriving to the United States, she searches for a way to keep her own identity and remember her people.

Weeks, S. (2000). *Regular Guy.* **New York: Harper Trophy.**

11-year-old Guy is convinced that his mother and father are too weird to be his biological parents. Buzz, Guy's friend, convinces him to search school records to locate another boy in school with the same birthday. Their results revealed that Bob-O, the weirdest kid in the class, has the same birthday as Guy. Guy and Bob-O decide to switch houses for a weekend to test his theory. Although Bob-O turns out to have ordinary parents, Guy's experiences help him begin to see his home life in a new light.

Waters, K. (2001). *Giving Thanks: The 1621 Harvest Feast.* **New York: Scholastic.**

This Thanksgiving story is one in a series of Scholastic books that view the roles of children in historical events through photographs of reenactments. This particular book alternates between the version of Thanksgiving that might have been told by the Indians and the version that might have been told by the European immigrants.

Werner, E.E. (1998). *Reluctant Witnesses: Children's Voices from the Civil War.* **Boulder, CO: Oxford Westview.**

The Civil War is seen through the eyes of children who participated in the war, and through the eyes of slave children.

Wiesner, D. (2001). *The Three Pigs.* **New York: Clarion.**

This book starts out like the traditional tale but gains new perspective when the pigs leave their story and wander around Storyland meeting other characters, eventually finding a dragon to accompany them home in order to keep the wolf away.

Wood, R.W. (2003). *Goodbye Vietnam.* **Memphis, TN: Omonomany.**

This book is a collection of short fictional remembrances of a Marine in Vietnam. It is fictional, although the author was a Marine during the Vietnam War.

Yolen, J. (2003). *My Brothers' Flying Machine: Wilbur, Orville, and Me.* **New York: Little, Brown.**

This account of the Wright brothers is told from the perspective of their younger sister, Katherine. The book includes information about the invention of the airplane and insights into the life of the Wright family.

CATEGORY TWO:
Social or Political Issues Between Individuals or Within Society

Bunting, E. (1991). *Fly Away Home*. **New York: Clarion.**
This picture book exposes the realities of a homeless father and son who live in an airport. The young child explains how to keep from being noticed when living in an airport. His ideas include sleeping sitting up and spending each night in a different area. Patterning reality, there is no set resolution to the little boy's dilemma.

Bunting, E. (1994). *Smoky Nights*. **San Diego, CA: Harcourt.**
In this Caldecott Award–winning book, Eve Bunting writes about the 1992 Los Angeles riots and how that experience helped neighborhood people move beyond their differences and form new relationships.

Bunting, E. (1998). *So Far from the Sea*. **New York: Clarion.**
Laura, a young girl, recounts her family's 1972 visit to the site of a camp in California, where her father and his parents were forced to stay during the Japanese-American Internment. The title is an allusion to the fact that the grandfather, who had been a fisherman before World War II, was prohibited from fishing during the Internment.

Dessen, S. (2000). *Dreamland*. **New York: Penguin Putnam Books.**
Caitlin's sister runs away from home and Caitlin begins to feel a sense of emptiness in her life. She meets a boy named Rogerson, who takes her mind off her sister. To her surprise, her relationship with Rogerson becomes dangerous and she can't seem to break free.

Fleischman, P. (1993). *Bull Run*. **New York: HarperCollins.**
This book tells the stories of sixteen people whose lives were affected by the Civil War. It reveals the painful experiences many people encountered during that battle and provides insights about war and its effects on everyday life.

Frank, A. (1993). *Anne Frank: The Diary of a Young Girl*. **New York: Prentice Hall.**
Anne's diary describes both the joys and torments of her daily life, in addition to typical adolescent thoughts. The diary covers the two years Anne and her family were in hiding during the Nazi occupation of Holland, before they were discovered and deported to concentration camps.

Franklin, P. (1995). *Melting Pot or Not? Debating Cultural Identity*. **Springfield, NJ: Enslow Publishers.**
The author argues that the United States is not a melting pot but a kaleidoscope. Emphasis is placed on various ethnic groups and their opinions in the ongoing debate about immigration and identity.

Garland, S. (1994). *I Never Knew Your Name*. **New York: Ticknor and Fields for Young Readers.**
A young boy tells the story of a teenage neighbor he has observed from a distance. The boy admires the teenager for his basketball skills and his love for animals. He sees him as an outcast disliked by his peers and is close to speaking to him but never does. One day the boy wakes up to the sound of an ambulance and finds out that the teenager has committed suicide.

Gold, A.L. (1997). *Memories of Anne Frank: Reflections of a Childhood Friend*. **New York: Scholastic.**
This book tells the story of Hannah Goslar, Anne Frank's best friend. The author recounts her relationship with Anne, her reactions to

the war, and effects of the war on her family, and Anne's disappearance. The horrors of the Holocaust are emphasized, as is the heroism of the prisoners in concentration camps.

Griffiths, A. (1992). *The Korean Americans.* **New York: Facts on File.**
This volume discusses the immigration of Koreans to the United States, with an emphasis on their experiences in trying to adjust to the demands of a heterogeneous society while trying to hold on to their own cultural identity.

Hesse, K. (1992). *Letters from Rifka.* **New York: H. Holt**
12-year-old Rifka and her family overcome political obstacles and face social issues in their migration from the Ukraine to Ellis Island.

Hesse, K. (2001). *Witness.* **New York: Scholastic.**
This book uses verse to reveal townspeoples' experiences and the effects of the Ku Klux Klan on people they viewed as their enemies.

Hidier, T. (2002). *Born Confused.* **New York: Scholastic.**
This story is about a teenage girl named Dimple who struggles with her own cultural identity as an Indian American living in New Jersey. When Dimple meets other people with similar issues, she becomes more comfortable with her identity and realizes that she is not alone.

Hoose, P. (2001). *We Were There, Too! Young People in American History.* **New York: Farrar, Straus and Giroux.**
This book reveals the active roles young people took during various periods of American history, ranging from the pre–Revolutionary era to more recent times.

Ippisch, H. (1996). *Sky: A True Story of Courage During WW II.* **New York: Simon & Schuster.**
Hanneke, a Dutch teenager, risked her life to help protect the Jews from the Nazis during World War II. After two years, she was discovered by the Germans and was sentenced to life in prison. Hanneke reminisces about the details of her experiences and tells the story as she remembers it.

Jacobs, F. (1992). *The Tainos: The People Who Welcomed Columbus.* **New York: G.P. Putnam.**
The author reveals the often untold side of the "discovery" of the Americas. The Taino people were the indigenous inhabitants of the Caribbean islands whose only records of existence have been letters of Columbus, Spanish explorers, and their own cave drawings. Columbus took these peaceful people as slaves and their culture virtually disappeared.

Jiang, J. (1997). *Red Scarf Girl: A Memoir of the Cultural Revolution.* **New York: Harper Trophy.**
This autobiography describes a family that wanted to follow Mao but suffered many indignities because the grandfather had been a landlord. Political relationships interweave with social relationships in a Chinese society characterized by extreme abuses of power.

Jones, C. (2002). *Every Girl Tells a Story: A Celebration of Girls Speaking Their Minds.* **New York: Simon & Schuster.**
Teenage girls speak their minds about their future. They discuss their hopes and dreams and what is required to obtain them.

Konigsburg, E. (1998). *The View from Saturday.* **New York: Simon & Schuster.**
Four sixth graders from Epiphany Middle School participate in the Academic Bowl to represent the school. Guided by their teacher, they become good friends and in the process learn the value of goals as well as of friendship.

Lowry, L. (1989). *Number the Stars.* **Boston: Houghton Mifflin.**
A 10-year-old Danish girl, Annemarie, and her family risk their own safety to help Annemarie's best friend and her Jewish family escape to Sweden, where they will be safe from the Nazis.

Lowry, L. *The Giver.* **(1993). Boston: Houghton Mifflin.**
In a society that is run by elders, 12-year-old Jonas is assigned the position of Receiver of Memory. Jonas becomes aware of the hypocrisy that rules the world while he is enriched with memories of a stimulating world.

Maynard, M. (1996). *Dreamcatcher.* **Vancouver, British Columbia, Canada: Raincoast Book Distribution.**
Fran moves away from the city with his mother and brother. He is challenged by the death of his father and the new man in his mother's life. Fran decides to adopt a raccoon and meets a girl named Jo who is struggling with her Native-American heritage. Through their experiences, they learn the importance of good friendship and of moving forward.

McDonald, J. (2000). *Shadow People.* **New York: Delacorte.**
Four teenagers are united by the rage they feel toward their overprotective parents, school authorities, and the system in general. This book is an excellent counter-text for well-adjusted high school students or for people who are actually drawn together by friendship rather than alienation.

McKissack, P. (1994). *Christmas in the Big House, Christmas in the Quarters.* **New York: Scholastic.**
On a Virginia plantation in 1859, the slaves work hard to get the big house ready for Christmas, and also to prepare their quarters for their own celebration. This story helps us see not only multiple views of Christmas but also the differences between the two ethnic groups and the power relationship that sustains that difference.

Naidoo, B. (2000). *The Other Side of Truth.* **New York: Harper Trophy.**
After their mother is murdered, two children are smuggled out of Nigeria to London. Their journalist father, the intended target of the murder, eventually joins them and is arrested for illegally emigrating. The author reveals many facts and contemporary issues about Africa through this story, which explores issues of family, exile, and freedom.

Park, L.S. (2002). *When My Name Was Keoko.* **New York: Clarion Books.**
A brother and sister struggle to hold fast to their national identity and traditions as the Japanese take over and oppress Korea during the World War II occupation of Korea by Japan. This is a fascinating study of the limits of human will and the all-encompassing nature of oppressive governments.

Sheldon, D. (1999). *Confessions of a Teenage Drama Queen.* **Massachusetts: Candlewick.**
It is Mary Elizabeth's first year in a new high school in suburban New Jersey. She becomes interested in the lead role for the annual play and competes with the most popular girl in the school for the part.

Speare, E.G. (1983). *Sign of the Beaver.* **Boston: Houghton Mifflin.**
In the Maine wilderness in the mid 1700s, 12-year-old Matt is left by his father to look after the cabin and newly planted crop while the father goes off to Massachusetts to collect the rest of the family and move them to the new homestead. Matt learns to hunt and survive with the help of Attean, the son of an Indian chief. In return, he teaches Attean to speak and read English by reading *Robinson Crusoe,* but Attean has a different interpretation of the story that lends itself to critical conversations.

Taylor, M.D. (1975). *Song of the Trees.* **New York: Bantam.**
A black family struggles against white racism during the 1930s in Mississippi. Although the book is not above criticism, Taylor successfully shows the subtle nature of discrimination against the blacks in the South at the time the story occurs.

Uchida, Y. (1996). *The Bracelet.* **New York: Puffin.**
Emi is a 7-year-old Japanese American who is sent to live in an internment camp with her mother and older sister. She realizes that she has lost the bracelet that her best friend, Laurie Madison, gave her as a keepsake, but she is not worried about it because she carries her friend in her heart.

Whelan, G. (2000). *Homeless Bird.* **New York: HarperCollins.**
Koly, an East Indian girl, gets married at age 13 and her husband of 16 promptly dies, leaving her widowed, unlikely to get a job and unable to marry again because of Indian customs. This book presents a view of Indian life from the perspective of a poor, homeless girl whose only misfortune is becoming widowed.

Wittlinger, E. (2002). *Gracie's Girl.* **New York: Alladin.**
Bess is upset with the fact that her mother spends all of her time in the soup kitchen. Bess becomes friends with Grace, an older homeless woman who reminds her of her grandmother. Through their experiences together, she learns a lot about herself and the world around her.

Yarbrough, C. (1996). *The Little Tree Growing in the Shade.* **New York: Putnam.**
An African-American family attends a "Roots of Rhythm and Blues" concert. At the concert, a father and his children discuss slavery, how their people held on to their cultural identity, and how they gained freedom.

Yep, L. (2001). *Lady of Ch'iao Kuo: Warrior of the South, China 531 A.D.* **New York: Scholastic.**
This story is about Lady Ch'iao Kuo, a teenage princess of the Hsien tribe in China. Lady Ch'iao keeps a diary that describes her role as a liaison between her tribe and the Chinese during times of both peace and war.

Yolen, J. (1996). *Encounter.* **San Diego: Harcourt.**
This story of Columbus's discovery of the island of San Salvador is told from the point of view of a young Taino. The boy, who is telling the tale as an old man, recalls that he warned his people to be wary of the newcomers. They ignored him and welcomed Columbus, an act that led to the destruction of the Tainos.

CATEGORY THREE:
Action Steps for Social Justice

Archer, J. (1996). *They Had a Dream: The Civil Rights Struggle from Frederick Douglass to Marcus Garvey to Martin Luther King, Jr., and Malcolm X.* **New York: Puffin.**
Discussions, speeches, and writings reveal the courage and determination of four leaders during the civil rights era.

Ashby, R., & Ohrn, D.G., eds. (1995). *Herstory: Women Who Changed the World.* **New York: Viking.**
This is a compilation of biographies that reveal contributions made to history by women, both familiar and unknown. These women discuss various careers in which they engaged, ranging from traditional "women's work" to nontraditional. Many women are represented whose lives had an impact on the world.

Ayer, E.H. (1995). *Parallel Journeys*. New York: Atheneum Books for Young Readers.
This dual biography of a Hitler Youth member and a Jewish girl who survives an Auschwitz death camp shows how they survive World War II and meet four decades later to work for peace and understanding. This book shows that transformation and change are possible.

Bang, M. (2000). *Nobody in Particular: One Woman's Fight to Save the Bay*. New York: Henry Holt.
Diane Wilson is a shrimper who takes on chemical plants that are poisoning the water where the shrimp live. This story tells about her many struggles and about the costs of taking action.

Bray, R.L. (1995). *Martin Luther King, Jr.* New York: Greenwillow.
This is a biography in picture-book format about Martin Luther King, Jr. Words and paintings tell the story of the contributions Dr. King made during a significant era in American history.

Coles, R. (1995). *The Story of Ruby Bridges*. New York: Scholastic.
A girl takes action as the first black child to attend a white school in New Orleans, Louisiana, in 1960.

Cronin D. (2000). *CLICK, CLACK, MOO: Cows That Type*. New York: Simon & Schuster.
Cows on a farm go on strike for warm blankets, and that leads to interesting negotiations with the farmer. This emphasizes the power of literacy and of taking action for what you believe in.

Lasky, K. (2002). *A Time for Courage: The Suffragette Diary of Kathleen Bowen*. New York: Scholastic.
Kathleen receives a diary and uses it to discuss the nation's battle for women's suffrage and World War I. The diary also reveals the life of a teenage girl who is trying to juggle school, friends, and family life during the struggle for women's rights.

Lewis, B., & Espeland, P. (1992). *Kids With Courage: True Stories About Young People Making a Difference*. Minneapolis, MN: Free Spirit.
Eighteen young people of various ethnic and economic backgrounds discuss what they perceive as crisis situations in their lives.

Liddington, J. (1999). *One Hand Tied Behind Us: The Rise of the Women's Suffrage Movement*. New York: Rivers Oram Press.
This book discusses suffragists from Britain who fought for equal pay, educational opportunities, and the right to work.

Loewen, N. (2002). *I Can Do It! Kids Talk About Courage*. Bloomington, MN: Picture Window Books.
In an advice-column format, this book describes the meaning of courage and discusses how it can be used in everyday situations.

Mochizuki, K. (1997). *Passage to Freedom: The Sugihara Story*. New York: Lee and Low.
This real-life account of Sugihara's life describes how he followed his conscience by issuing travel visas and saved the lives of numerous Jews during World War II.

Rappaport, D. (2000). *Freedom River*. New York: Jump at the Sun/Hyperion Books for Children.
An ordinary businessman risks his life and liberty to free others from slavery via the Underground Railroad. This book shows that ordinary people can and do take noble action toward social justice.

Appendix C: Websites to Use When Teaching Critical Literacy

Websites That Provide Additional Information About Critical Literacy

English Learning Area: Critical Literacy

http://www.discover.tased.edu.au/english/critlit.htm

This website, which is maintained by the Tasmanian Office of Education, clarifies concepts and practices of critical literacy and provides abundant resources.

Critical Analysis Using Clever Cloze

http://www.myread.org/guide_cloze.htm

In this website sponsored by the Australian government, there is a step-by-step example of how to implement critical literacy through analysis and the cloze procedure. Examples from a newspaper and student activities help orient the teacher to think about how to help students raise issues, such as how words are used to empower or disempower certain groups, and how mood is used to give power.

Journal for Pedagogy, Pluralism, & Practice

http://www.lesley.edu/journals/jppp/4/shor.html

Ira Shor, an expert in critical literacy, explains it from his perspective in the *Journal for Pedagogy, Pluralism & Practice.*

National Council of Teachers of English

http://www.ncte.org

The National Council of Teachers of English has information about critical literacy that is easy to find using the search button on the NCTE website.

Reading Online

http://www.readingonline.org and click on "search"

The International Reading Association's online journal *Reading Online* has a very productive search engine that yields refereed journal articles about critical literacy.

Websites to Use as Resources When Planning Critical Literacy Lessons

AMERICAN REVOLUTION

The History Place—American Revolution

http://www.historyplace.com/unitedstates/revolution

The American Revolution is addressed from early Colonial America to the English Colonial Era to the war for independence and the birth of a nation.

National Society of Sons of the American Revolution

http://www.sar.org/

This website provides information about the American Revolution, emphasizing military actions and different theaters. Information specifically for students is also featured.

LIBERTY! The American Revolution

http://www.pbs.org/ktca/liberty

This website chronicles the events of the American Revolution and is a companion to the PBS series LIBERTY! The American Revolution.

Americanrevolution.org

http://www.americanrevolution.org/

Historical content and more than a thousand links to additional information are featured on this website.

THE CIVIL WAR

The American Civil War Homepage

http://sunsite.utk.edu/civil-war/

This website offers information about the Civil War, including music of the era, women of the Civil War, cartoons, battlefields, the roles of various states, dignitaries, presidents, and officers of the armies.

Civil War Index Page

http://www.homepages.dsu.edu/jankej/civilwar/civilwar.htm

This website provides links to information about a variety of Civil War–related topics.

The Civil War Homepage

http://www.civil-war.net/

This website offers contacts and links to databases including photos and official records.

HOMELESSNESS

Help the Homeless

http://www.hud.gov/kids/hthsplmn.html

Explanations of who homeless people are, where they are, and what kids and adults can do to help the homeless are featured on this site.

National Coalition for the Homeless

http://www.nationalhomeless.org/

This site presents the mission statement, breaking news, hot topics, and facts about the National Coalition. Additional features of this site include legislation and policy, projects, speakers, conferences, Internet sources, educational materials, and publications.

Institute for the Study of Homelessness and Poverty at the Weingart Center

http://www.weingart.org/institute/

This site provides information about the purpose of this institute. Additional featured areas include Just the Facts, Latest Publications and Websites, and Latest Contacts.

IMMIGRATION

Center for Immigration Studies

http://www.cis.org/

Current news articles about immigration and links to a variety of related topics are featured on this site. History, legal and illegal immigration, refugees, and asylum are among the related links. Topics of sample articles include security, monitoring, and diversity.

American Immigration

http://www.bergen.org/AAST/Projects/Immigration/

Numerous links about American immigration are provided, including reasons for immigration, methods of transportation and ports of arrival, places where immigrants settled, and effects and impact on America. Other links include information on Ellis Island, quotations about immigration, and news groups.

American Family Immigration History Center

http://www.ellisisland.org/default.asp

This site offers access to immigration records and the option to inscribe a name on the American Immigration Wall of Honor.

Immigration: Stories of Yesterday & Today

http://teacher.scholastic.com/immigrat/

This Scholastic site features an interactive tour of Ellis Island, immigrant stories of yesterday and today, an oral history scrapbook, research prompts, and a teacher's guide.

NATIVE AMERICANS

NativeWeb

http://www.nativeweb.org/

This site offers insights into Native-American culture through history and current events.

The American West—Native Americans

http://www.americanwest.com/pages/indians.htm

This website provides information about resources, education, artwork, and movies about Native Americans.

Native American Home Pages

http://www.nativeculture.com/lisamitten/indians.html

This website, maintained by a Mohawk Indian, provides links to Native-American nations and organizations.

The Wild West: Cherokee, Apache, Navajo, Cheyenne, and Pueblo

http://www.thewildwest.org/native_american/

Information about the legends, societies, places, art, and religion of the Native-American people is presented.

TOLERANCE

Tolerance.org

http://www.tolerance.org/

This site offers links for teachers, parents, teens and kids, as well explorations of current issues. For example, in October the site featured a young adult commentary on the inappropriateness of celebrating Columbus Day.

SPLCENTER.ORG

http://www.splcenter.org/

This site of the Southern Poverty Law Center offers an Intelligence Project, Teaching Tolerance. This site sponsors the Civil Rights Memorial and tells how people can help.

International Tolerance Network

http://\/www.tolerance-net.org/news/index.html

This International Network site includes featured links, such as new publications, newsletters, new manuals, participation in modern society, and new Anti-Defamation League programs for children, among others. This site also includes other links on topics of tolerance.

THE UNDERGROUND RAILROAD

National Underground Railroad Freedom Center

http://www.undergroundrailroad.org/

This is an interactive website that offers students the opportunity to discover what life was like on the Underground Railroad.

The Underground Railroad

http://www.nationalgeographic.com/railroad/

National Geographic provides students with the opportunity to take an interactive journey on the Underground Railroad.

Aboard the Underground Railroad

http://www.cr.nps.gov/nr/travel/underground/

The National Register of Historic Places offers students an opportunity to travel to places on the Underground Railroad and read about people involved.

WOMEN'S ROLES IN WORLD WAR II

American Women and World War II

http://www.scc.rutgers.edu/njh/WW2/ww2women/womenintro.htm

Rutgers University maintains this site, which emphasizes the role of the women from the state of New Jersey in World War II.

Rosie the Riveter

http://www.rosietheriveter.us/

This website details the history of women's roles in factories manufacturing planes, ships, and automobiles for the war effort.

Cary Academy Library—Pathfinders—World War II

http://web1.caryacademy.org/library/pathfinders/ww2.htm

This website provides a timeline with images, events, and descriptions of women's involvement in World War II.

WOMEN'S SUFFRAGE

History of Women's Suffrage

http://www.rochester.edu/SBA/history.html

This website tells the history of the women's suffrage movement. In addition to Susan B. Anthony and Elizabeth Cady Stanton, the work of many other suffragists who influenced the movement is also included.

Women's Suffrage

http://teacher.scholastic.com/researchtools/researchstarters/women/article5.htm

This site emphasizes the struggle women have experienced to achieve equal rights. In the United States, conflicts between feminists contributed to the creation of two organizations. These two groups united and became the National American Women Suffrage Association, which fought for and obtained the right to vote in 1920. In addition, Great Britain's and other countries' struggles to achieve women's rights to vote are highlighted.

Not For Ourselves Alone: The Story of Elizabeth Cady Stanton and Susan B. Anthony

http://www.pbs.org/stantonanthony/

This website reveals the history and contributions of Elizabeth Cady Stanton and Susan B. Anthony through historic documents and essays.

The History of Women's Suffrage

http://www2.worldbook.com/features/whm/html/whm010.html

The history of women's suffrage is highlighted on this website. The story of how women's suffrage began, the rise of the movement, as well as women's suffrage in other countries are emphasized.

WORLD WAR II

Resource Listing for WWII

http://www.ibiblio.org/pha/

Information about the attack on Pearl Harbor and the Japanese and European theaters is provided.

BBC—History—World War II

http://www.bbc.co.uk/history/war/wwtwo/index.shtml

Information about Great Britain's role in World War II is featured, including a link for children that provides information about British children's experiences on the home front.

American Aces of World War II

http://www.acepilots.com/

This website is dedicated to the role of pilots and airplanes in World War II.

The History Place—Holocaust Timeline

http://www.historyplace.com/worldwar2/holocaust/timeline.html

This website presents a timeline of events from 1933, when Hitler was appointed Chancellor of Germany, to 1961, when Adolf Eichmann went on trial in Israel for war crimes.

A Cybrary of the Holocaust, Remember.org

http://www.remember.org

Resources for researching World War II and the Jewish people's plight can be found on this site.

United States Holocaust Museum

http://www.ushmm.org

Information about the Holocaust Museum, education, research, and remembrance is available on this site.

The Holocaust History Project

http://www.holocaust-history.org

This site provides archives of documents, photographs, recordings, and essays about the Holocaust.

References

Adelaide Declaration on National Goals for Schooling in the Twenty-First Century (1999). Available at http://www.curriculum.edu.au/mceetya/nationalgoals/natgoals.htm

Au, K. (1998). Social constructivism and the school literacy learning of students of diverse backgrounds. *Journal of Literacy Research*, 30: 297-319.

Australian Association for the Teaching of English (AATE) and the Australian Literacy Educators Association (ALEA) (2002). "My Read: Strategies for Teaching Reading in the Middle Years." Retrieved Jan. 21, 2004, from http://www.myread. org/guide_cloze.htm

Baker, L., & Wigfield, A. (1999). Dimensions of children's motivation for reading and their relations to reading activity and reading achievement. *Reading Research Quarterly*, 34 (4), 452-481.

Brooks, J.G. & Brooks, M.G. (1993). *In Search of Understanding: The Case for Constructivist Classrooms.* Alexandria, VA: Association for Supervision and Curriculum Development.

Cambourne, B. (2002). Holistic, integrated, approaches to reading and language arts instruction: The constructivist framework of an instructional theory. In A. Farstrup & J. Samuels (Eds.), *What research has to say about reading instruction* (3rd ed., pp. 25-47). Newark, DE: International Reading Association.

Comber, B. (2001a). Classroom explorations in critical literacy. In H. Fehring & P. Green (Eds.), *Critical literacy: A collection of articles from the Australian Literacy Educators' Association* (pp. 90-102). Newark, DE: International Reading Association.

Comber, B. (2001b). Critical literacies and local action: Teacher knowledge and a "new" research agenda. In B. Comber and A. Simpson (Eds.), *Negotiating critical literacies in classrooms* (pp. 271-282). Mahwah, NJ: Erlbaum.

Cummins, J., & Sayers, D. (1995). *Brave new schools: Challenging cultural illiteracy through global learning networks.* New York: St. Martin's Press.

de Bono, E. (1985). *Six thinking hats.* Boston: Little, Brown.

Durkin, D. (1978-1979). What classroom observations reveal about reading comprehension instruction. *Reading Research Quarterly*, 14, 481-533.

Durrant, C., & Green, B. (2001). Literacy and the new technologies in school education: Meeting the literacy challenge. In H. Fehring & P. Green (Eds.), *Critical literacy: A collection of articles from the Australian Literacy Educators'* *Association* (pp. 142-164). Newark, DE: International Reading Association.

Edelsky, C. (Ed.) (1999). *Making justice our project: Teachers working toward critical whole language practice.* Urbana, IL: National Council of Teachers of English.

Fehring, H., & Green, P. (Eds.). (2001). *Critical literacy: A collection of articles from the Australian Literacy Educators' Association.* Newark, DE: International Reading Association.

Freire, P. (1970). *Pedagogy of the oppressed.* New York: Continuum.

Freire, P. (1983). The importance of the act of reading. *Journal of Education*, 165, 5-11.

Freire, P. (1998). *Teachers as cultural workers: Letters to those who dare to teach.* Boulder, CO: Westview.

Gambrell, L.B. (1996). Creating classroom cultures that foster reading motivation. *The Reading Teacher*, 50(1), 14-25.

Gambrell, L.B., Palmer, B.M., Codling, R.M., Mazzoni, S.A. (1996). Assessing motivation to read. *The Reading Teacher*, 49(7), 518-533.

Gee, J.P. (1996). Social linguistics and literacies (2nd ed.). London: Taylor and Francis.

Gee, J.P. (2000). Discourse and sociocultural studies in reading. In M. Kamil, P. D. Pearson, & R. Barr (Eds.), *Handbook of reading research* (Vol.3, pp. 195-207). Mahwah, NJ: Erlbaum.

Gee, J.P. (2001). Reading as situated language: A sociocognitive perspective. *Journal of Adolescent and Adult Literacy*, 44(8), 714-725.

Green, P. (2001). Critical literacy revisited. In H. Fehring and P. Green (Eds.), *Critical literacy: A collection of articles from the Australian Literacy Educators' Association* (pp. 7-14). Newark, DE: International Reading Association.

Guthrie, J.T., & Wigfield, A. (1997). *Reading engagement: Motivating readers through integrated curriculum.* Newark, DE: International Reading Association.

Harris, T.L., & Hodges, R.E. (Eds.). (1995). *The literacy dictionary: The vocabulary of reading and writing.* Newark, DE: International Reading Association.

Harvey, S. & Goudvis, A. (2000). *Strategies that work.* York, Maine: Stenhouse Publishers.

Janks, H. (1993a). *Language and position.* Johannesburg, South Africa: Hodder & Stroughton.

Janks, H. (1993b). *Language, identity, and power.* South Africa: Hodder and Stoughton.

Leistyna, P., & Woodrum, A. (1996). Context and culture: What is critical pedagogy? In P. Leistyna, A. Woodrum, & S.A. Sherblom (Eds.) *Breaking free: The transformative power of critical pedagogy.* Cambridge, MA: Harvard Educational Review Reprint Series.

Leistyna, P., Woodrum, A., & Sherblom, S.A. (Eds.) (1996). *Breaking free: The transformative power of critical pedagogy.* Cambridge, MA: Harvard Educational Review Reprint Series.

Lewison, M., Flint, A. S., & Van Sluys, K. (2002). Taking on critical literacy: The journey of newcomers and novices. *Language Arts* 79(5) 382-392.

Luke, A. (2000). Critical literacy in Australia. *Journal of Adolescent and Adult Literacy*, 43(5), 448-461.

Luke, A., & Freebody, P. (1999). Further notes on the four resources model. *Reading Online.* Retrieved March 15, 2002 from http://www.reading.org/publications/ROL/.

Machado, A. (1982). Proverbios y cantares. In A. Trueblood (trans.), *Antonio Machado: Selected poems*, p. 142. Cambridge, MA: Harvard University Press.

McCarthy, S.J., & Moje, E.J. (2002). Identity matters. *Reading Research Quarterly*, 37, 228-238.

McLaughlin, M. (2001). *Sociocultural influences on content literacy teachers' beliefs and innovative practices.* Paper presented at the 51st Annual Meeting of the National Reading Conference, San Antonio, TX.

McLaughlin, M. (2000). Inquiry: Key to critical and creative thinking in the content areas. In M. McLaughlin & M.E. Vogt (Eds.), *Creativity and innovation in content area teaching* (pp. 31-54). Norwood, MA: Christopher Gordon.

McLaughlin, M., & Allen, M.B. (2002a). *Guided comprehension: A teaching model for grades 3–8.* Newark, DE: International Reading Association.

McLaughlin, M., & Allen, M.B. (2002b). *Guided comprehension in action: Lessons for grades 3–8.* Newark, DE: International Reading Association.

McLaughlin, M., & DeVoogd, G. (2004). Critical literacy as comprehension: Expanding reader response. *Journal of Adolescent and Adult Literacy.*

Meyer, M. (2001). Between theory, method, and politics: Positioning of the approaches to CDA. In R. Wodak and M. Meyers (Eds.), *Methods of Critical Discourse Analysis.* Thousand Oaks, CA: Sage.

National Council of Teachers of English, & International Reading Association. (1996). *Standards for the English Language Arts*. Available at: http://www.reading.org/advocacy/elastandards/standards.html

O'Brien, J. (2001). Children reading critically: A local history. In B. Comber and A. Simpson (Eds.), *Negotiating critical literacies in classrooms* (pp. 37-54), Mahwah, NJ: Erlbaum.

Pearson, P.D. (2001). *What we have learned in 30 years*. Paper presented at the 51st Annual Meeting of the National Reading Conference, San Antonio, TX.

Rabelais, F. (1991). *Gargantua and Pantagruel*. New York: W. W. Norton. (Original book published in 1554.)

Rosenblatt, L. M. (1978). *The reader, the text, and the poem: The transactional theory of the literary work*. Carbondale, Illinois: Southern Illinois University Press.

Rosenblatt, L. M. (1980). What facts does this poem teach you? *Language Arts*, 57(4), 386-394.

Rosenblatt, L. M. (1994). The transactional theory of reading and writing. In R.B. Ruddell, M. R. Ruddell, & H. Singer (Eds.), *Theoretical models and processes of reading* (4th ed., pp. 1057-1092). Newark, DE: International Reading Association.

Rosenblatt, L.M. (2002, December). *A pragmatist theoretician looks at research: Implications and questions calling for answers*. Paper presented at the 52nd annual meeting of the National Reading Conference, Miami, FL.

Shannon, P. (2001, April). New literacies in action: What's a fellow to do? Family literacy at this time in this place. *Reading Online*, 4(9). Available: http://www.readingonline.org/newliteracies/lit_index.asp?HREF=/newliteracies/action/shannon/index.html

Short, K.G., Harste, J.C., & Burke, C. (1996). *Creating classrooms for authors and inquirers*. Portsmouth, NH: Heinemann.

Smith, P. (2003). *Critical media*. Paper presented at the meeting of the 48th Annual Convention of the International Reading Association, Orlando, FL.

Van Sluys, K. (2003). *Engaging in critical literacy practices in a multiliteracies classroom*. Paper presented at the 53rd Annual Meeting of the National Reading Conference, Scottsdale, AZ.

Vasquez, V. (2003). *Getting beyond "I like the book."* Newark, DE: International Reading Association.

Vygotsky, L. (1978). *Mind in society: The development of higher psychological processes*. Cambridge, MA: Harvard University Press.

Wink, J. (2000). *Critical pedagogy: Notes from the real world*. (2nd ed.). New York: Longman.

Wodak, R. (2001). What CDA is about. In R. Wodak and M. Meyers (Eds.), *Methods of Critical Discourse Analysis*. Thousand Oaks, CA: Sage.

LITERATURE

Angelou, M. (1998). *Life Doesn't Frighten Me*. New York: Stewart, Tabori & Chang.

Bambara, T.C. (2002). "Raymond's Run." In *The Language of Literature Grade 8*. Boston: McDougall Littell.

Bang, M. (2000). *Nobody in Particular: One Woman's Fight to Save the Bay*. New York: Henry Holt.

Brokaw, T. (1998). *The Greatest Generation*. New York: Greenwillow.

Brown, M. (1982–2000). *The Arthur the Aardvark* series. Boston: Little, Brown and Company.

Bunting, E. (1991). *Fly Away Home*. New York: Clarion.

Bunting, E. (1994). *Smoky Night*. San Diego, CA: Harcourt.

Bunting, E. (1999). *A Picnic in October*. New York: Harcourt Brace.

Busby, P. (2003). *First to Fly: How Wilbur and Orville Wright Invented the Airplane.* New York: Crown Publishers.

Carroll, A. (Ed.). (2001). *War Letters: Extraordinary Correspondence from American Wars.* New York: Scribner.

Celsi, T. (1990). *The Fourth Little Pig.* Austin, TX: Steck Vaughn Company.

Choi, Y. (2001). *The Name Jar.* New York: Knopf.

Coles, R. (1995). *The Story of Ruby Bridges.* New York: Scholastic.

Cronin D. (2000). *CLICK, CLACK, MOO: Cows that Type.* New York: Simon & Schuster.

Dallet, N. (1986). *Seaport Summer: In Their Own Words —Oral Histories of Ellis Island Immigrants.* 30-34.

de Kay, J.T. (2001). *Meet Christopher Columbus.* New York: Random House.

Fast, H. (1986). *Seaport Summer. The World Within a Nation.* 20-21.

Farris, C.K. (2002). *My Brother Martin: A Sister Remembers Growing Up With the Rev. Dr. Martin Luther King, Jr.* New York: Simon and Schuster.

Fleischman, P. (1993). *Bull Run.* New York: HarperCollins.

Frank, A. (1993). *Anne Frank: The Diary of a Young Girl.* New York: Prentice Hall.

Gold, A.L. (2000). *A Special Fate: Chiune Sugihara, Hero of the Holocaust.* New York: Scholastic.

Grimes, N. (2002). *Talkin' About Bessie.* New York: Scholastic.

Hantover, J. (1986). *Seaport Summer: Listening to the Ghosts of Ellis Island.* 25–28.

Hesse, K. (1992). *Letters from Rifka.* New York: H. Holt.

Hest, A. (1999). *When Jessie Came Across the Sea.* New York: Scholastic.

Hobbs, W. (1997). *Bearstone.* New York: Harper Trophy.

Hoyt-Goldsmith, D. (2001). *Celebrating Ramadan.* New York: Holiday House.

Hyman, T.S. 1986. *Little Red Riding Hood.* New York: Holiday House.

Jacques, B. (1986). *Redwall.* New York: Ace.

Jacobs, F. (1992). *The Tainos: The People Who Welcomed Columbus.* New York: G.P. Putnam.

Jiang, J. (1997). *Red Scarf Girl: A Memoir of the Cultural Revolution.* New York: Harper Trophy.

Kikhler-Zilberman, L. (1990). *My Hundred Children.* New York: Dell Laurel-Leaf.

Levine, E. (1994). *If Your Name Was Changed at Ellis Island.* New York: Scholastic.

Lowry, L. (1989). *Number the Stars.* Boston: Houghton Mifflin.

Macaulay, D. (1990). *Black and White.* Boston: Houghton Mifflin.

Maestro, B. (1996). *Coming to America.* New York: Scholastic.

McKissack, P. (1994). *Christmas in the Big House, Christmas in the Quarters.* New York: Scholastic.

Mochizuki, K. (1995). *Baseball Saved Us.* New York: Lee and Low.

Muñoz Ryan, P. *Esperanza Rising.* (2000). New York: Scholastic.

Na, A. *Step from Heaven.* (2003). New York: Puffin.

Naidoo, B. (2000). *The Other Side of Truth.* New York: Harper Trophy.

Pfister, M. (1996). *The Rainbow Fish.* Trans. by J. A. James. New York: North South.

Rappaport, D. (2001). *Martin's Big Words.* New York: Hyperion Books for Children.

Reimers, D. (1986). *Seaport Summer.* New York: An immigrant city, 17-19.

Ringgold, F. (1999). *If a Bus Could Talk: The Story of Rosa Parks.* New York: Simon & Schuster.

Roop, P. & Roop, C. (2000). *Christopher Columbus.* New York: Scholastic.

Rowling, J.K. (1998). *Harry Potter and the Sorcerer's Stone*. New York: Scholastic.

Rowling, J.K. (1999). *Harry Potter and the Prisoner of Azkaban*. New York: Scholastic.

Ryan, P.M. (2000). *Esperanza Rising*. New York: Scholastic.

Scieszka, J. (1992). *The Stinky Cheese Man and Other Fairly Stupid Tales*. New York: Viking.

Scieszka, J. (1989). *The True Story of the 3 Little Pigs!* New York: Penguin.

Seuss, Dr. (1957). *The Cat in the Hat*. New York: Random House.

Shannon, D. (1998). *No, David!* New York: Scholastic.

Shihab-Nye, N. (1999). *Habibi*. New York: Simon Pulse.

Simon, S. (2000). *Wolves*. HarperCollins Juvenile Books.

Silverstein, S. (1964). *The Giving Tree*. New York: Harper & Row.

Snicket, L. (1999). *The Bad Beginning: A Series of Unfortunate Events, Book One*. New York: HarperCollins.

Soto, G. (2000). "Seventh Grade." In *Prentice Hall Literature: Timeless Voices, Timeless Themes*. (pp. 122-127). Upper Saddle River, NJ: Prentice Hall.

Taylor, M.D. (1974). *Song of the Trees*. New York: Skylark.

Turner, A. (2003). *Love Thy Neighbor: The Tory Diary of Prudence Emerson, Green Marsh, Massachusetts, 1774*. New York: Scholastic.

Van Allsburg, C. (1991). *The Wretched Stone*. Boston: Houghton Mifflin.

Whelan, G. (2000). *Homeless Bird*. New York: HarperCollins.

Wiesel, E. (1982). *Night*. New York: Bantam Books.

Wiesner, D. (1999). *Sector 7*. New York: Clarion Books

Wiesner, D. (2001). *The Three Pigs*. New York: Clarion Books.

Winthrop, E. (1985). *The Castle in the Attic*. New York: Bantam.

Wood, R.W. (2003). *Goodbye, Vietnam*. Memphis, TN: Omonomany.

Woodruff, E. (1999). *The Memory Coat*. New York: Scholastic.

Woodruff, E. (2000). *The Orphan of Ellis Island*. New York: Scholastic.

Yolen, J. (1992). *Encounter*. New York: Harcourt Brace.

Index

Rowling, J.K., (*Harry Potter and the Sorcerer's Stone*), 45-46

Ryan, Pam Muñoz (*Esperanza Rising*), 47

S

Sassaman, Jennifer, 35, 128-32

say something, 45

Sayers, D., 15

school curriculums and critical literacy, 29
  grade levels, 32
  multiple modes of expression, 32
  multiple types of text, 32
  national standards, 30-31
  situated, social learning, 32
  state standards, 31
  subject areas, 31
  technology integration, 32

Scieszka, Jon,
  (*The Stinky Cheese Man and Other Stupid Fairly Tales*), 48
  (*The True Story of the 3 Little Pigs!*), 122-24

seeing beyond the text (defined), 152

semantic map, 77-78, 129

Seuss, Dr. (*The Cat in the Hat*), 56

Shannon, David (*No, David!*), 67-72, 124-28

Shannon, P., 151

Sherblum, S.A., 23, 150

Short, K.G., 45

Sillivan, Susan, 135-39

Silverstein, Shel (*The Giving Tree*), 41-45

Simon, Seymour (*Wolves*), 37, 39-40

Smith, P., 57

Snicket, Lemony (*The Bad Beginning*), 47-48

social constructivist theory 21, (defined) 152

social justice and social action (defined), 152

Soto, Gary ("Seventh Grade"), 133-35

Standards for the English Language Arts, 30

strategies to teach critical literacy, 38-54
  alternative perspectives, 39-40, 49-53
  defined, 150
  problem posing, 41-48, 61-87, 125
  teaching a strategy, 39-40

switching, 47-48, 92, 140-41

T

Taylor, Mildred D. (*Song of the Trees*), 25-27

teachers' reflections, 146

terms, glossary of critical literacy, 150-52

text selection
  action steps for social justice (books that focus on), 56-57
  disrupt the commonplace and provide multiple viewpoints (books that), 54-56
  social or political issues (books that focus on), 56
  trade books to use when teaching critical literacy, 153-63
  websites to use when teaching critical literacy, 164-67

theme-based focus groups, 52-53

trade books to use when teaching critical literacy, 153-63

transactional theory and reader stance, 21-23

Turner, A. (*Love Thy Neighbor*), 17

V

Van Allsburg, Chris (*The Wretched Stone*), 82-85

Van Sluys, K., 15, 16, 17-18, 54

Vasquez, Vivian (*Getting Beyond "I like the book"*), 32, 151

Vygotsky, L., 21

W

websites
  additional information on critical literacy, 164
  planning and teaching critical literacy, for, 164-67

Whelan, Gloria (*Homeless Bird*), 47

White, Denise, 67-72, 124-28

Wiesel, Elie (*Night*), 56

Wiesner, David (*Sector 7*), 57, (*The Three Pigs*), 56

Wink, J., 23, 150

Winthrop (*Castle in the Attic*), 47

Woodrum, A., 23, 150

XYZ

Yolen, Jane (*Encounter*), 128-32, 135-39